NORTH CAROLINA

2005 NCAA CHAMPIONS

THE NEWS&OBSERVER

newsobserver.com

Life enriched.

SP
SPORTS
PUBLISHING
L.L.C.

www.SportsPublishingLLC.com

D1717125

Publishers

Peter L. Bannon and Joseph J. Bannon Sr.

Senior Managing Editors

Joseph J. Bannon Jr. and Susan M. Moyer

Coordinating Editor

Noah A. Amstadter

Developmental Editor

Travis W. Moran

Art Director

K. Jeffrey Higgerson

Photo Editor

Erin Linden-Levy

Book Design

Dustin Hubbart

Cover Design

Joseph Brumleve

Project manager, book layout

Kathryn R. Holleman

Imaging

K. Jeffrey Higgerson, Kenneth J. O'Brien, Dustin Hubbart, and Heidi Norsen

President/Publisher

Orage Quarles III

Sr. V.P./Executive Editor

Melanie Sill

Editorial Page Editor

Steven Ford

Managing Editor

John Drescher

Public Editor

Ted Vaden

Sr. V.P./Finance

George McCanless

V.P./Classified Advertising

Durwood Canaday

V.P./Human Resources

Jackie Stark

V.P./Marketing

Felicia Gressette

Sr. V.P./Advertising

Alan Truax

V.P./Display Advertising

Jim McClure

V.P./Operations

Richard Rinehart

V.P./Interactive Media

Gary Smith

Soft cover ISBN: 1-59670-257-2 • Hard cover ISBN: 1-59670-131-5

Front and back cover photos:

Contents

Preseason 8

Kentucky 12/4 12

Georgia Tech 1/12 18

Jawad WIlliams 24

Wake Forest 1/15 26

Duke 2/9 32

Rashad McCants 38

UConn 2/13 40

North Carolina State 2/22 . . . 46

Sean May 52

Maryland 2/27 54

Raymon Felton 60

Florida State 3/3 62

Marvin Williams 68

Duke 3/6 70

ACC Tournament Game 1 . . . 78

ACC Tournament Game 2 . . . 80

NCAA Game 1 84

NCAA Game 2 86

NCAA Game 3 90

NCAA Game 4 96

Roy Williams 102

NCAA Game 5 106

NCAA Championship 114

Regular Season Statistics . . .126

Regular Season Results 127

Newspaper Credits 128

Fran Carruthers (left) and UNC freshmen Kennedy Carruthers (center) and Merrill McCarty cheer during a pep rally for the Tar Heels Sunday night, March 27, 2004, at the Dean E. Smith Center. Staff Photo by Juli Leonard

Publisher's Note

Dear Reader,

Happy days are here again for Tar Heel basketball fans. Their beloved 'Heels have returned to glory, winning the NCAA title to cap a season that began with great expectations and delivered on them. The sky is Carolina blue once again.

As they celebrate this true blue victory, fans surely will be thankful for the leadership and savvy of Coach Roy Williams and the skills, athleticism, and determination of his team. They, and we, applaud the achievements of this talented team and its victorious coach.

The News & Observer and newsobserver.com have covered every step of the journey, from the first practice to the final buzzer. We're pleased to offer this book, which draws upon our longstanding commitment to world-class coverage of ACC basketball. In these pages, you'll see dramatic photographs of key plays, emotional moments, and season highlights. You'll relive the season as you read the game stories and commentary of our talented staff.

We hope you'll enjoy every page.

Orage Quarles III
President and Publisher

ABOVE: UNC fans Tanner Fort, 12, left, and Aaron Likness, 10, right, try to get autographs from the Tar Heels before practice at the Charlotte Coliseum on Thursday the day before Oakland took on UNC at the NCAA tournament Syracuse Regional opening round. Staff photo by Scott Lewis

UNC'S "BLUE" PERIOD MAY BE HISTORY

By ROBBI PICKERAL

When Georgia Tech's Jarrett Jack dribbled around Rashad McCants last March to hit the winning shot in the quarterfinals of the ACC Tournament, it was a snapshot of what's still missing from North Carolina: smart defense, consistent communication, and something harder to define—mystique.

Which is why, despite all of the hype and hope around campus that UNC basketball "is back," men's coach Roy Williams said, "I don't know that I believe it, myself."

At least, not yet.

Yes, the No. 4 Tar Heels boast five starters returning from last season.

Yes, they returned to the NCAA Tournament last season after a two-year hiatus.

And, yes, Williams exited a recent practice thinking, "My golly, we're going to be pretty doggone good"—something he said he never uttered after a workout last season.

But Williams, who returned to his alma mater last season after 15 years at Kansas, is not just trying to rebuild a team that has three seniors still driven by the memories of an 8-20 season.

He's trying to restore an aura still bruised by two years of losses and letdowns.

"I do think that they can reach that mystique again and that all of the players are in place for that to happen," said former Tar Heels point guard Phil Ford, now an assistant coach with the Detroit Pistons. "...But I think it takes time; that's not something that happens overnight."

The Carolina mystique was not just about baby blue, wins, and a long tradition. The mystique is the steely belief by those adorned in light blue that Carolina will win, no matter the adversity.

ABOVE: Roy Williams will have plenty of returning talent to work with for this upcoming season. From left: Rashad McCants, Sean May, Raymond Felton, Jawad Williams, and Jackie Manual. Staff Photo by Scott Lewis

ABOVE: Melvin Scott is hoisted and twirled around by C.J. Hooker, left, Marvin Williams, and Jackie Manuel during their rendition of "Flashdance" at the antic-filled Late Night with Roy celebration at the Smith Center. Staff Photo by Shawn Rocco

Down eight points with 17 seconds? No problem. The Heels came back against Duke in 1974.

Need a clutch shot? Michael Jordan's championship-winning jumper against Georgetown is the most famous among many.

Ford used to notice how long it took opposing teams to yank their starters, even if they were winning by double figures in the closing minutes. Foes knew, Ford said, that if the Heels had a glimmer of hope, "We'd take advantage of it."

"There was a quiet confidence when I was a player and I was a coach," said Ford, who played at Carolina from 1974-1978 and later was an assistant coach, said. "I always thought as a player that if we did what Coach [Dean] Smith, Coach [Bill] Guthridge, and Coach [Eddie] Fogler told us to do, we'd win, because there was nothing that could happen on the basketball court that we weren't prepared for."

That still seemed to be missing from Carolina last season.

UNC lost a stunning nine games last season with 90 seconds to play—including that game against the Yellow Jackets in the ACC Tournament when the Heels came back from an 11-point deficit but couldn't finish.

Carolina also lost to Duke 83-81 in overtime when it allowed Chris Duhon to drive down the court for a lay-up.

There also were embarrassing setbacks, such as Florida State's 24-point comeback in Tallahassee and a 82-71 loss at Clemson in which the Tar Heels looked disinterested.

There were some flashbacks of past glory, such as when swingman Rashad McCants made a winning three-pointer to topple top-ranked Connecticut.

"At times last year, we were really good," Williams said. "We beat Connecticut once, we beat Georgia Tech once, we took Duke down to the wire, and that's three of the four teams that were in the Final Four....

"And I think the second year in any style of play—the trust, the confidence, the familiarity that you have is going to make it better there, too."

After a season of teaching fundamentals, Williams now expects those basics to turn into habits, which in turn will result in more wins.

The pieces for revival appear to be in place, with juniors Sean May, McCants, and Felton back and freshmen forward Marvin Williams and point guard Quentin Thomas adding depth.

But Williams is careful to remind followers that the Tar Heels lack what he calls the "successful experience" of other ACC foes such as Georgia Tech and Wake Forest. In other words, those programs return players with more NCAA Tournament experience.

He also stresses that defense is key.

So it is how those pieces now fit together—and how much these Tar Heels have faith in their coaches and themselves when the game is on the line—that could determine whether they add consistent success to their experience.

And whether they start to exhibit the once-familiar Carolina mystique.

"It's not going to be one game, it's not going to be the tournament in Maui," Williams said. "It's going to be a very successful year, and the forecast would be for another successful year the following year. What Coach Smith, the standard he set here—I tried to do the same thing at Kansas, and I felt like we did a pretty good job for 15 years, and I think at least the last 14, I thought we had a chance to win the whole dad-gum thing, and that's what I want to get here."

WAYS TO WIN

By ROBBI PICKERAL

Every time the ball glided toward the basket at Smith Center, North Carolina forwards Jawad Williams and David Noel shared a similar thought process:

Find No. 44.

Box out No. 44.

Limit No. 44.

The result: Six lowly rebounds for No. 44, Chuck Hayes, Kentucky's leading scorer and rebounder; a 51-30 rebounding edge for No. 9 Carolina; and an easy 91-78 victory over the No. 8 Wildcats.

UNC's players now begin studying for final exams with a six-game winning streak.

"They were more aggressive," said Hayes, who was in foul trouble early and was one of three Wildcats to foul out late. "They just wanted it more, I guess."

On the backboards and off.

During a game in which Kentucky (4-1) never led and never really threatened, Carolina (6-1) showed why swingman Rashad McCants is already mentioning St. Louis—the site of the Final Four—in his post-game comments.

Center Sean May grabbed 19 rebounds, thanks in part to his tall teammates keeping Hayes away from the ball. Nine Tar Heels played at least nine minutes, showing improved depth. The Tar Heels shot 49.2 percent, led by McCants's 28 points.

And after playing seven games in 16 days, "I think there's hope for us defensively," said coach Roy Williams, whose team held Kentucky to 42.9 percent shooting. "I think a lot of times last year I thought we had no hope."

OPPOSITE PAGE: UNC's David Noel steals the ball from Kentucky's Joe Crawford during second half action in the Dean Smith Center at Chapel Hill, NC. The Heels beat the Wildcats 91-78. Staff Photo by Chuck Liddy

"They came in with a good game plan."

—Chuck Hayes
Kentucky forward

One of those times was likely after last season's loss at Kentucky, when four Tar Heels were benched for a stretch. Roy Williams said Wednesday that he remembered it as, "the least competitive, the least focused, the least energized of any team I've ever had going into a big environment."

Competitiveness, focus, and energy were not a problem this time.

Before the game, there was much talk about the fact that no current UNC player had beaten Kentucky, which had won four straight against the Tar Heels. But Noel, who shared the duty of guarding Hayes with starter Jawad Williams, said there was just as much talk about slowing Kentucky's best senior, who Roy Williams called one of his favorite players.

"We knew we had to box him out, and every time we wanted to find him and box him out and keep him off the boards, because he gets so many second-chance points that it don't make no sense," said Noel, who had 10 points and five rebounds off the bench. "He'll miss a shot, then miss another shot, then get another rebound, then make another basket. So we wanted to prevent that."

That was fairly easy early, as Hayes got into foul trouble by picking up his second infraction with 13:05 left in the first half. By that time, the quick-running, ball-stripping Tar Heels had a 22-6 lead. And Hayes could only watch from the bench for the rest of the half as the Wildcats cut it to 10 twice, only to be halted by three-point plays each time.

"It just took him out of things," Kentucky coach Tubby Smith said of Hayes's foul trouble. "He was really pumped up to play. His game is all about being physical, aggressive, and rebounding. I'll have to watch the film to see if he was really fouling as much as they say he was fouling."

Hayes was back on the floor to open the second half, and got his first field goal with 14:44 left, which cut Kentucky's deficit to 57-48. The Wildcats chipped to within six on their next possession, when Kelenna Azubuike made a 3-pointer. But they never got any closer, thanks to a combination of bad Wildcat shots and UNC's quick transition game.

Hayes, who began the afternoon averaging 13.8 points and 11 rebounds, was 2-for-7 in the game, all in the second half. And while all six of Hayes's rebounds came after halftime, they mattered little, considering 10 of May's came after halftime, as well.

OPPOSITE PAGE: UNC's head coach Roy Williams yells at game officials during first-half action in the Dean Smith Center at Chapel Hill. Staff Photo by Chuck Liddy

"[Limiting Hayes] played a big part of it, because we kept him off the offensive glass so Sean was able to get a lot of defensive boards," said Jawad Williams, who finished with 19 points and seven rebounds.

He said controlling Hayes was a group effort—just like the victory.

"I've got to give them credit, their coaching staff credit," Hayes said. "They came in with a good game plan."

OPPOSITE PAGE: UNC's Jackie Manuel goes to the floor to steal the ball from Kentucky's Kelenna Azubuike during first half action in the Dean Smith Center at Chapel Hill, North Carolina. Staff Photo by Chuck Liddy

BELOW: UNC's Marvin Williams and Jackie Manuel team up against Kentucky's Josh Carrier for a first half steal. Staff Photo by Chuck Liddy

	1st	2nd	Total
Kentucky	32	46	78
North Carolina	47	44	91

KENTUCKY

Player	FGM-A	3FGM-A	FTM-A	O-D REB	A	BLK	S	TP
44 Hayes	2-7	0-0	0-0	2-4	2	4	1	4
24 Azubuike	10-19	4-6	0-0	2-4	2	0	5	24
33 Morris	2-9	0-0	3-6	2-4	2	1	0	7
4 Rondo	3-4	0-0	1-3	0-0	2	0	3	7
22 Sparks	3-10	1-7	2-2	0-1	5	0	1	9
10 Obrzut	0-1	0-0	0-0	0-0	0	0	0	0
13 Perry	1-4	1-2	0-0	0-0	0	0	0	3
32 Crawford	4-8	1-5	2-5	3-2	1	0	0	11
3 Bradley	4-6	2-3	0-0	0-1	3	0	0	10
21 Alleyne	0-0	0-0	0-0	0-3	0	4	1	0
5 Carrier	0-0	0-0	0-0	0-0	0	0	0	0
2 Moss	1-2	1-2	0-0	0-0	2	0	0	3

NORTH CAROLINA

Player	FGM-A	3FGM-A	FTM-A	O-D REB	A	BLK	S	TP
21 J. Williams	6-9	0-1	7-8	2-5	1	0	0	19
42 May	6-11	0-0	2-5	5-14	4	1	0	14
5 Manuel	3-6	0-0	3-3	2-2	0	0	3	9
32 McCants	7-15	4-7	10-11	2-2	1	1	2	28
2 Felton	0-5	0-1	3-9	0-5	7	0	1	3
24 M. Williams	2-5	1-1	0-0	1-3	0	0	1	5
34 Noel	4-4	0-0	2-4	2-3	1	0	1	10
1 Scott	1-4	1-3	0-0	0-0	0	0	0	3
11 Thomas	0-0	0-0	0-0	1-1	1	0	1	0

DISMANTLING THE HIVE

By ROBBI PICKERAL

It's no secret that North Carolina coach Roy Williams believes in defense. He preaches persistence. He wants consistency. He expects greatness.

Yet there his team was at the Smith Center, showing again during a 91-69 rout of No. 8 Georgia Tech why sometimes the best defense in the world—or at least the Atlantic Coast Conference—doesn't really matter.

When that defense—in this case Georgia Tech's—is trying to handle the No. 3 Tar Heels (14-1, 3-0 ACC).

The Yellow Jackets, who began the game as the league leaders in field goal percentage defense and 3-point field goal percentage defense, held UNC to 41.2 percent and 40.9 percent, respectively, in those categories. It was the first time in seven games the Tar Heels, who have now won 14 straight, didn't make at least 50 percent of their shots.

Problem was, Tech's (11-3, 2-1) dogged defense—which Williams said is still better than UNC's—couldn't make up for the fact that it was without injured star guard B.J. Elder; that it missed its first 13 3-point attempts; and that it was out-rebounded by 19, including 12 on the offensive boards.

"I thought we did a great job on the backboards; we had 15 more possessions than they did in the first half," Williams said.

And although, Williams added, the Tar Heels converted five points from offensive rebounds in the first half, the most important point was that they had 15 more opportunities to score than the Jackets.

OPPOSITE PAGE: Georgia Tech's Luke Schenscher, left, is tied up under his basket by UNC's Sean May, center, and Jackie Manuel, right, in the first half of play.
Staff Photo by Corey Lowenstein

Opportunities for point guard Raymond Felton to bury one of his three 3-pointers or hand out one of his seven assists.

Opportunities for forwards Jawad Williams (18 points) and Marvin Williams (14 points) to score inside and out.

Opportunities for center Sean May to get to the free-throw line, where he was 6-for-6 with 12 points plus 13 rebounds for the game.

Co-leading scorer Rashad McCants, who had a career-high four blocks, was in foul trouble early, so he didn't get as many opportunities as usual. But UNC's firepower is so deep, it didn't even matter.

Get the drift?

"That's the thing—everyone on their team can score. They're a great offensive team," Georgia Tech center Luke Schenscher said.

"They could be the best team in the country," said Yellow Jackets coach Paul Hewitt, whose bench picked up a technical foul in the second half. "Them, Illinois and Wake Forest, from what I've seen on tape, in my opinion, might be the three best teams."

Tech, which was also missing reserve Ra'Sean Dickey to an injury, actually led once, when forward Isma'il Muhammad made the second of two free throws. That made it 1-0.

But the advantage didn't last long.

Not only did the Jackets get bashed around on the offensive boards, but also they looked as if they had greased their hands with vegetable oil before

"Everyone on their team can score."

—Luke Schenscher
Georgia Tech center

the game because they had major problems holding onto the ball.

Within the first eight minutes, they had already committed nine turnovers while making only one field goal. Meanwhile, UNC took its first double-figure lead, 17-5, when Felton followed Tech's sixth consecutive turnover with a corner 3.

Tech never caught up, despite intensifying its defense in the second half. UNC led 46-28 at the break and by as many as 25 points before it was all over.

"I let the guys talk after the game; I didn't talk," Hewitt said. "Because they realize that when you allow a team to get 17 offensive rebounds in the first half...that's a pretty grim stat. That comes down to just heart and really going after it.

"They got us. They got to the ball quicker than us."

The Jackets have now played three ranked teams this season; they have lost to all three.

OPPOSITE PAGE: Jawad Williams and Raymond Felton contain Georgia Tech's Jarrett Jack during the Tar Heels' 91-69 win at the Dean Smith Center. Staff photo by Scott Lewis

"They could be the best team
in the country."

—Paul Hewitt

Georgia Tech Head Coach

For UNC, meanwhile, the victory sets up a much-anticipated showdown against fourth-ranked Wake Forest in Winston-Salem. It will be the first time in history the Tar Heels and Demon Deacons have met while both are ranked in the top five of The Associated Press poll.

Still, Roy Williams said, "I want to enjoy this game. Georgia Tech is a big-time team. I feel good about this."

Especially considering his team's defense—the one he'd like to see be tops in the ACC, if not the country—held the Jackets to 36.8 percent shooting.

OPPOSITE PAGE: UNC's Raymond Felton, right, keeps teammate Jawad Williams focused during the Tar Heels' 91-69 win over Georgia Tech. Staff Photo by Scott Lewis

BELOW: UNC's starters, taken out with less than two minutes to play, erupt on the bench in the final seconds of their matchup against Georgia Tech. UNC won 91-69.
Staff Photo by Corey Lowenstein

	1st	2nd	Total
Georgia Tech	28	41	69
North Carolina	46	45	91

GEORGIA TECH

Player	FGM-A	3FGM-A	FTM-A	O-D REB	A	BLK	S	TP
2 Muhammed	4-7	0-0	3-9	0-6	0	0	2	11
55 McHenry	0-2	0-2	0-0	0-4	0	1	1	0
12 Schenscher	5-9	0-0	3-4	5-3	3	5	0	13
3 Jack	6-14	2-4	10-10	0-8	1	0	4	24
11 Bynum	3-10	0-4	4-6	0-1	1	0	1	10
23 Morrow	1-6	0-4	4-5	0-0	0	1	2	6
44 Tarver	0-1	0-0	0-0	0-0	0	0	3	0
5 West	1-5	0-1	0-0	1-1	1	0	1	2
35 Frederick II	0-2	0-1	0-0	0-0	2	0	0	0
14 Jones	1-1	1-1	0-0	0-0	0	0	0	3

NORTH CAROLINA

Player	FGM-A	3FGM-A	FTM-A	O-D REB	A	BLK	S	TP
21 J. Williams	6-10	1-3	5-6	0-3	2	0	0	18
42 May	3-11	0-0	6-6	4-9	3	0	1	12
5 Manuel	1-8	0-1	0-1	5-0	2	0	0	2
32 McCants	4-7	1-2	3-5	0-5	3	4	0	12
2 Felton	3-11	3-8	2-2	1-6	7	3	3	11
24 M. Williams	3-7	1-2	7-8	3-3	0	0	2	14
34 Noel	3-3	1-1	0-2	1-1	1	0	1	7
1 Scott	3-8	2-5	0-0	0-1	2	0	2	8
11 Thomas	0-1	0-0	0-0	0-1	3	0	0	0
3 Terry	0-0	0-0	1-2	0-1	0	0	0	1
41 Sanders	0-0	0-0	0-0	0-0	0	0	0	0
0 Holley	1-1	0-0	1-2	0-0	1	0	1	3
15 Everett	0-0	0-0	0-0	0-0	0	0	0	0
22 Miller	0-0	0-0	0-0	0-0	0	0	0	0
35 Hooker	1-1	0-0	1-1	0-1	0	0	0	3

#21 JAWAD WILLIAMS

By A.J. Carr

Amid the resounding din in the Dean Smith Center, Jawad Williams says he can distinguish one voice from the thousands of others.

It's his mother's.

Gail Hillmon-Williams is usually shouting for her son to "box out!" or "move!" or "rebound!"

The North Carolina senior forward has learned to listen to his mother, a former Cleveland State basketball player. She hasn't steered him wrong so far.

Her 6-foot-9 son is enjoying his best season, with 16.6 points per game, 62.7 percent shooting overall, and 42.9 percent accuracy from three-point range for the sixth-ranked Tar Heels.

Things have changed for the better since last season, when he struggled with injuries, and since the early part of his collegiate career, when he considered leaving UNC.

As a freshman in 2001-02, Williams was carrying the seniors' bags, the team was struggling toward a dismal 8-20 record, and he wasn't happy about his playing time.

"It was depressing," he says. "I wanted to go back toward home and [transfer], maybe to Cincinnati."

His mother intervened.

"I told him I didn't feel that was an option," says Gail, who travels to Chapel Hill about twice a month and wears a replica of Jawad's No. 21 jersey at games. "He made a commitment, and I told him, 'Carolina will be there for you. We will work through it.'"

After an auspicious start last season, a concussion and broken nose sent his performances spiraling downward.

Playing with a mask for nearly six weeks obstructed his vision, made him tentative and eroded his confidence. He'd laugh when teammates called him "Hannibal Lector," but his game suffered.

"[The mask] affected me a lot," says Williams, who was making about 57 percent of his shots before the concussion and wound up shooting 45.8 percent. "Biggest thing was I lost confidence."

Williams still keeps the mask in his locker, not as a memento but in case he needs it again. But now "I'm injury-free," he says, knocking on a wooden desk.

During Carolina's 14-2 start, Williams was the team's most dependable player. Williams gets points posting up, stroking shots from behind the arc, sprinting on the fast break and attacking the offensive glass.

"From preseason, he has been our most consistent player," Carolina coach Roy Williams says. "He was on the way to a big-time year last year. But you've got to be healthy to play this game. Now he is more comfortable, knows more of what I want, and the year of familiarity [in our system] is helping."

It was a matter of time, Jawad Williams says, before he regained his aim and confidence.

"I knew what I could do. I worked over the summer and figured it was time for me to come out of that shell," Williams says.

As for his ACC-best shooting, he says, "my teammates are getting me the ball in good spots, and I don't take many bad shots."

Williams grew up in Cleveland in a "gym-rat" family. His father and brother, Tony, were Gold Glove boxers. One sister, Nasheema, played basketball at Vanderbilt and professionally. Another, Siedah, is starring at Virginia, and a third, Adjoni, is a big scorer on a Cleveland high school team.

Gail Williams, a probation officer, allowed her children to choose their own activities. But she insisted on giving them "unique" names and liked Jawad, an Arabic name that means "open-handed generosity and kindness," because it "sounded smooth."

As productive as he has been, he's not the first player who generally comes to mind on a team that features Rashad McCants, Sean May, and Raymond Felton. He's not necessarily even the first Williams who comes to mind, now that freshman Marvin Williams has arrived.

"Jawad is soft-spoken, lets the actions speak for themselves," May says. "For that reason, he slides under the radar. People talk about Rashad, Raymond, and me."

But Williams is Carolina's leader, "point-blank," teammate David Noel says. "He's done everything imaginable

Name: Jawad Williams
Born: February 19, 1983
Hometown: Cleveland, Ohio
Attended: St. Edwards High School
 (Lakewood, OH)
Position: Forward
Height: 6 foot 9
Weight: 218 pounds

Staff Photo by Robert Willett

we could ask—scoring, rebounding, all the necessary things."

His multi-dimensional game is getting attention from pro scouts, although Williams, a power forward at UNC, may be better suited to playing as a small forward in the NBA.

"He's gotten better every year," Sacramento Kings scout Keith Drum says. "He's developed his range shooting, has become more consistent, and defensively has done well. He's fallen into a group like a lot of guys, a 4-man [power forward] in college, but might have to adjust to more of a 3-man.

"For him, there will be an adjustment defensively, guarding guys 20 feet away from the goal on a consistent basis. Offensively, he's proven he can shoot outside. His next step will be using his ballhandling, creating his own shot."

Drum says that playing on such a talented team also is helping prepare Williams.

"He's not being overlooked," Drum says. "He will get his opportunities."

C.P.'S BETTER THIS TIME

By ROBBI PICKERAL

The chant began with less than seven minutes left in the first half, shortly after Wake Forest point guard Chris Paul made two free throws:

"C.P.'s better! C.P.'s better!"

And by the end of No. 4 Wake Forest's 95-82 win over No. 3 North Carolina at Joel Coliseum, even Tar Heels point guard Raymond Felton had to agree.

"I didn't do exactly what he did, because he did his job, and his team got a win," said Felton, whose team's 14-game winning streak was snapped.

"And I feel like I didn't do my job tonight, because we didn't win."

In a nationally televised match-up hyped for the showdown of two of the nation's top point guards, neither Felton nor Paul disappointed the raucous sellout crowd.

However, a disappointed Felton described his 16-point, five-assist, two-turnover performance as "pretty good," while Paul's game-high 26-point, eight-assist, six-rebound, one-turnover output as "great."

"I wasn't taking it personal, but coach always says this is a team game played by individuals," said Paul, who has now scored at least 20 points in four of his last seven games. "He always tells you, 'you have to beat your guy; you have to beat the match-up between you and your guy.' And that's what you have to do."

And that's what he did.

While Felton struggled offensively early—making only one of his three first-half three-pointers and only two of his eight first-half shots—Paul

OPPOSITE PAGE: Wake Forest's Taron Downey pressures UNC's Melvin Scott as the Demon Deacons win 95-82. Downey came off the bench to help the Deacons win.
Staff photo by Scott Lewis

pushed the pace en route to a 43-33 half-time lead. Thirteen of his 15 first-half points came during a 26-16 run that turned a 17-17 deadlock into a 10-point lead for Wake.

It marked the first time the Tar Heels have trailed at half-time since their season-opening loss at Santa Clara.

Felton tried to pick up his—and his team's—pace in the second half. Problem was, unlike all of UNC's former opponents this season, Paul was able to keep up, and also get back on defense, against the junior who he recently referred to as the fastest guard in the country.

He was also able to counter Felton on the scoreboard, when the speedster tried to make a surge.

For instance, with 10:01 left, Felton drove the lane, got fouled, converted the three-point play and cut his team's deficit to 64-55. But Paul came back at the speed of, well, Paul, streaking down the court and converting a short floater.

Comeback thwarted.

Later, with 5:46 left, Felton scored on a reverse to cut it to 73-65. But Paul was there again, scoring on a drive and this time converting a three-point play of his own.

"You have to beat your guy; you have to beat the match-up between you and your guy."

—Chris Paul
Wake Forest point guard

Comeback thwarted again.

"He can weave down and use people, his own teammates, and rub off people…it's a little like a great broken-field runner in football," UNC coach Roy Williams said.

"…Chris has the ability to get to the basket and finish a play. He's slight of build. He's not Arnold Schwartzenegger, but he might be of heart."

When Paul wasn't scoring, he was passing—such as his assist to center Eric Williams with 2:23 left that gave Wake an 85-75 advantage.

That thwarted another, final, UNC comeback try.

And got the crowd chanting again:

"C.P.'s better! C.P.'s better!"

OPPOSITE PAGE: Wake Forest's Jamaal Levy pulls in a rebound over UNC's Sean May during the Demon Deacons' 95-82 win over the Tar Heels. Staff Photo by Scott Lewis

ABOVE: UNC coach Roy Williams reacts to a foul call against the Tar Heels during their 95-82 loss to Wake Forest.
Staff Photo by Scott Lewis

LEFT: UNC head coach Roy Williams talks to Rashad McCants as McCants heads to the bench with his fourth foul during the Tar Heels' 95-82 loss to Wake Forest. Despite playing only 20 minutes, McCants led the Heels with 19 points.
Staff Photo by Scott Lewis

OPPOSITE PAGE: UNC's Rashad McCants drops his head after missing the first of two free throws during the final minutes of the Tar Heels' 95-82 loss to Wake Forest.
Staff Photo by Scott Lewis

"He has an excellent work ethic; he's a student of the game," said Wake coach Skip Prosser, who insisted he wouldn't trade his sophomore point guard for anything. "He also can read and can watch TV. So he knew the magnitude of the challenge for him today, and I think, by and large, he stepped up to it."

	1st	2nd	Total
North Carolina	33	49	82
Wake Forest	43	52	95

NORTH CAROLINA

Player	FGM-A	3FGM-A	FTM-A	O-D REB	A	BLK	S	TP
21 J. Williams	3-8	2-6	4-4	2-1	3	0	1	12
42 May	3-9	0-0	3-3	4-5	0	0	1	9
2 Felton	5-18	1-7	5-7	0-2	5	1	3	16
5 Manuel	1-2	0-1	0-0	1-1	2	0	0	2
32 McCants	8-12	0-2	3-5	0-1	1	1	0	19
1 Scott	0-3	0-1	0-0	0-0	1	0	0	0
3 Terry	1-2	1-2	0-0	0-0	0	0	0	3
11 Thomas	0-0	0-0	0-0	0-0	0	0	1	0
24 M. Williams	4-6	1-2	6-6	3-4	0	1	0	15
34 Noel	2-7	2-4	0-1	2-6	3	0	0	6

WAKE FOREST

Player	FGM-A	3FGM-A	FTM-A	O-D REB	A	BLK	S	TP
10 Levy	1-5	0-0	4-4	1-7	1	3	1	6
13 Danelius	2-5	1-2	6-6	5-2	0	2	0	11
31 Williams	4-6	0-0	0-0	1-3	0	0	1	8
1 Gray	3-12	3-9	4-4	1-0	2	0	1	13
3 Paul	8-18	1-2	9-9	1-5	8	0	5	26
0 Ellis	3-4	1-1	4-4	2-1	0	1	1	11
4 Downey	5-9	3-6	5-5	0-4	1	0	1	18
33 Strickland	0-2	0-1	0-0	1-3	2	0	1	0
55 Visser	1-1	0-0	0-0	0-0	0	0	0	2

COACH K COURT AT CAMERON INDOOR STADIUM IN DURHAM, NC

DEVILS DEFEND TURF

By LUCIANA CHAVEZ

In a one-possession battle between Duke, the Atlantic Coast Conference's best defense, and North Carolina, the nation's best offense, defense won.

Duke led throughout the second half but was clinging to a 71-70 lead with the clock ticking down on the final 30 seconds in a jam-packed Cameron Indoor Stadium.

But the Blue Devils gave the ball back to the Tar Heels in a manner they wouldn't have guessed. The shot clock was near zero when J.J. Redick launched a long three-point attempt from the top of the key.

Air ball.

With the Duke crowd demanding a stop and the small UNC contingent praying for a bucket, Carolina point guard Raymond Felton dribbled down the court guarded by Duke senior Daniel Ewing.

A brief opening in the lane closed up, and Felton picked up his dribble.

Seeing teammate Rashad McCants covered by Redick, Felton tried to squeeze the ball to David Noel along the sideline in front of the UNC bench.

Noel had the ball for a second before Duke freshman DeMarcus Nelson forced him to lose the ball out of bounds as time expired.

"We were trying to go to Rashad and when Raymond came off, [Raymond] was wide open but didn't take the shot," Noel said. "He kind of got trapped a little bit so it came to me. I turned, Nelson knocked the ball loose and the clock hit zero."

"Both of our captains were guarding guys who would have taken the last shot," Duke guard Sean Dockery said of Redick guarding McCants and Ewing guarding Felton. "We didn't want either of them to get the last shot."

Neither did.

"I really thought we were in good shape," UNC coach Roy Williams said.

OPPOSITE PAGE: Duke's Daniel Ewing, rear, and UNC's Raymond Felton, bottom, go for the ball in the second half of play. Staff Photo by Ethan Hyman

It was a game that the Blue Devils had to have for their ACC season and the Tar Heels needed to win for their sanity.

"Our team has been mentally tough all year," Duke coach Mike Krzyzewski said. "They have never made excuses about injuries or depth or anything like that. They've really shown up to play every game."

The Devils have won 15 of the last 17 meetings between the two teams. Duke (18-2) and UNC (19-3) are now tied atop the ACC standings at 8-2.

UNC center Sean May, who had game highs of 23 points and 18 rebounds, kept the Tar Heels close with power play after power play inside.

But Duke still led 71-66 with 1:54 remaining.

That five-point lead nearly wasn't enough as May tipped in McCants's missed three-pointer at the 1:12 mark.

McCants, who shot 3-for-13 from the floor, scored just his third basket of the game 18 seconds later. He made a driving layup with 54 seconds left.

But the Tar Heels would never get a chance to attempt a winning shot.

"I'm proud of the way our team fought their way back in," Williams said.

The Tar Heels played from behind throughout the game and couldn't run like they usually do. After trailing by seven at halftime while shooting 10-for-30 from the field, UNC turned up the volume on the game while making 15 of 27 shots in the second half.

Duke held on behind its defense and by hitting 9 of 10 free throws in the final nine minutes of the game.

In North Carolina's two conference losses, Wake Forest and Duke combined to shoot 53-for-54 from the free-throw line.

Redick scored 18 points but Nelson's 16 points and four steals off the bench—in place of Shavlik Randolph—gave Duke a strong presence when it needed it.

Carolina trailed at halftime for just the fourth time this season, including during all three of its losses.

One of the most dangerous fastbreak teams in college basketball managed just two fastbreak points in the game as both sides played physical ball from the opening tip.

In fact, the first play of the game after the tipoff turned into a full-court scramble for a loose ball.

You could practically hear the gears grinding against each other on both sides of the court as defense dictated the action.

Duke led 10-2 with Redick and Ewing hitting early threes, but McCants and Felton combined for 11 early points as the Heels turned Duke's lead into a 15-12 North Carolina advantage with 11:56 left in the half.

But Felton and McCants would have little impact on offense for the rest of the half.

OPPOSITE PAGE: UNC's Roy Williams talks with Rashad McCants in the first half during Duke's 71-70 victory at Cameron Indoor Stadium. Staff Photo by Ethan Hyman

Though Duke hit several long threes early, those dried up quickly when the Heels successfully began pushing the Devils out of their offense. Duke's guards weren't having any luck driving to the basket.

The Devils couldn't get near the paint until Nelson, a former quarterback, started muscling in. He fed Shelden Williams on two straight buckets inside to give Duke a 20-19 lead with 6:33 left in the half.

OPPOSITE PAGE: UNC's Rashad McCants can't believe it after he fouled Duke's DeMarcus Nelson in the second half during Duke's 71-70 victory at Cameron Indoor Stadium. Staff Photo by Ethan Hyman

BELOW: Duke's Mike Krzyzewski talks with UNC's Rashad McCants and Raymond Felton after Duke's 71-70 victory at Cameron Indoor Stadium. Staff Photo by Ethan Hyman

	1st	2nd	Total
North Carolina	29	41	70
Duke	36	35	71

NORTH CAROLINA

Player	FGM-A	3FGM-A	FTM-A	O-D REB	A	BLK	S	TP
21 J. Williams	1-6	0-1	0-0	2-1	2	1	0	2
32 McCants	3-13	1-8	4-4	1-1	1	0	0	11
42 May	8-14	0-0	7-7	5-13	2	2	0	23
2 Felton	5-10	2-4	1-3	0-3	3	0	2	13
5 Manuel	3-4	0-0	3-4	5-1	0	0	1	9
1 Scott	0-0	0-0	0-0	0-0	0	0	0	0
11 Thomas	0-0	0-0	0-0	0-0	0	0	0	0
22 Miller	0-0	0-0	0-0	0-0	0	0	0	0
24 M. Williams	5-8	0-0	2-5	1-4	1	1	1	12
34 Noel	0-2	0-1	0-0	1-0	1	0	0	0

DUKE

Player	FGM-A	3FGM-A	FTM-A	O-D REB	A	BLK	S	TP
23 Williams	3-6	0-0	5-6	2-7	2	5	5	11
42 Randolph	1-4	0-0	2-2	1-3	1	1	2	4
4 Redick	4-12	4-10	6-6	0-4	1	0	2	18
5 Ewing	5-16	3-9	2-2	0-1	3	0	0	15
15 Dockery	1-3	0-1	2-2	1-1	2	0	3	4
13 Melchionni	1-5	1-3	0-0	1-1	0	0	1	3
21 Nelson	5-10	2-2	4-4	2-0	3	0	4	16
51 Johnson	0-0	0-0	0-0	0-0	0	0	0	0

#32 RASHAD McCANTS

By Robbi Pickeral

North Carolina basketball player Rashad McCants does not wear his heart on his sleeve.

He wears it on his feet.

In all, more than three dozen sets of initials, nicknames, symbols, and sayings adorn McCants's size 13s. They are the junior swingman's comfort shoes, in more ways than one.

"I just wanted to have something on the court to remind me of why I'm still playing basketball," he said recently, "and why I'm trying to be the best at it."

That the 6-foot-4, 207-pound Asheville native has to be reminded says something about his tempestuous times at UNC. Since the day his dad wrote "4-12-86 next Michael Jordan" in one-year-old Rashad's baby book, basketball has been McCants's passion; besides writing poetry, it's all the 20-year-old ever has wanted to do.

McCants, who describes himself as "private," admits that he's difficult to get to know.

"Just because people can't figure me out, they want to bash me for some reason," he said quietly, shaking his head.

It's little wonder that before the season McCants had four words tattooed to each arm.

On his right: "Born to be hated."

On his left: "Dying to be loved."

"Rashad, I think, really does want the fans to love him," said his mom, Brenda Muckelvene. "He would like to come out from under that cloud. He would like to start over with a fresh, clean slate and say, 'Let the games begin.'"

With his innate athletic ability and a body sculpted by early years on a football field, McCants has been a beacon for attention ever since he was a quiet, introspective kid starring on a neighborhood basketball court. His mom's favorite snapshot is of McCants flying above a basketball rim at 11 years old.

His father, James, kept him focused on success by stressing academics, manners, and hard work.

"He always said, 'You can always be in a corner selling drugs; you can be in the recreational parks playing basketball, washed up; or you can be playing in the NBA. It's your decision,'" said McCants, who played at Asheville's Erwin High before transferring to New Hampton (N.H.) Prep for his last two seasons.

When he bought his non-team-issued, Nike Air Huaraches the day before the season-opener at Santa Clara, the first thing he wrote on them was a favorite line from the Bible.

"I think the first Scripture that came to my mind was, 'If God is with us, who can be against us?'" McCants said. "And that just made a lot of sense to me, the situation I was in, everybody was pretty much scrutinizing and saying things, all the negative articles. I was just saying to myself, 'If He's with me, then nobody should be against me.'"

These days, No. 32 grants very few one-on-one interviews and ponders his words carefully in postgame media sessions. Often, he pauses before responding.

"I always tell my friends and my mother and father that I don't open my mouth and say anything unless I really feel like I'm right," said McCants, who has two younger sisters. "If I'm wrong, I really won't say anything, because I hate the embarrassment of being wrong, and the bad judgment."

Teammates say some of McCants's headline-inducing incidents have been blown out of proportion because Rashad is, well, Rashad.

They accept him and wish others would, too.

"I told him, if I were to say, 'Carolina is like being in prison,' nobody would have read into it," center Sean May said. "...But a lot of that is on him, with the way he carries himself and the way he acts on the floor sometimes. He's the type of player, he demands respect with the way he plays, but a lot of times people don't give him that respect because of the statements that he makes and the emotions that he shows. We've talked about that.

"Is that fair? No. Is that the reality? Yes."

Name: Rashad McCants
Born: September 25, 1984
Hometown: Asheville, North Carolina
Attended: New Hampton Prep (NH)
Position: Guard / Forward
Height: 6 foot 4
Weight: 207 pounds

Staff Photo by Scott Lewis

McCants found a kindred spirit in former UNC star Rasheed Wallace, who has generated his own share of scorn because of his penchant for technical fouls and his perceived attitude problems.

"He told me we were very similar as far as the way we carry ourselves," McCants said. "...When he's around his friends, everyone knows how cool he is; he's the best guy in the world. But people that don't know him don't think that way because they can never figure him out.

"And that's, I think, why we're so similar, because we don't give people a chance to figure us out because we already have our friends and we already have people close to us."

Yet, McCants hasn't been living as much of a loner existence this season as he has in past years.

"Now, he's really fun to be around," May said. "I think it shows out on the floor, because there are times when he

goes up for a shot and passes it, where last year he would have just shot it even if it didn't have a 50 percent, 40 percent chance of going in. Now, he doesn't care about his numbers. He's looking out for his teammates, and you can see that by him not trying to go out there and get 30 every night."

Roy Williams laughingly said he even accepts his players' penchant for writing on their game shoes, as long as "Williams RIP" doesn't end up on any sneakers.

Still, McCants, who often is described with adjectives such as "mercurial" and "enigmatic" by the national media, knows he has plenty to prove and to improve upon, including defense, ball-handling, and his midrange game. When he does leave Carolina, he said, he wants to be described and remembered as one thing above all else: "a winner."

HEELS BOUNCE BACK

By ROBBI PICKERAL

No one on North Carolina's basketball team blamed point guard Raymond Felton for the Tar Heels' one-point loss at Duke.

No one except Felton himself.

"I felt like I let my team down," he said, referring specifically to the final possession of the game, when he passed up an opportunity to drive toward the basket, picked up his dribble too soon, threw an awkward pass to the play's fifth option and watched in despair as David Noel fumbled the ball out of bounds as time expired.

So during the second half of No. 2 UNC's 77-70 victory over No. 19 Connecticut at Hartford Civic Center, the speedy playmaker did what he failed to do against the Blue Devils: He took advantage of every available opening.

With the score knotted at 48-48 and 12:51 remaining, the junior scored eight points (including two three-pointers), grabbed two rebounds, had a steal and a turnover during an 18-7 run that gave UNC (20-3) a commanding 11-point lead.

Defending national champion UConn (15-6) led by as many as seven points in the first half, out-rebounded the Tar Heels by 12, and blocked 16 shots.

But the Huskies never caught up after Felton's spurt.

"Raymond was still, I think, feeling the effects of the other night," said UNC coach Roy Williams, adding that he felt about "179 degrees" better than he did after the Duke loss.

"...I really thought in a stretch of about five minutes, every time there was a loose ball, Raymond came up with it."

OPPOSITE PAGE: In the second half, UNC's Raymond Felton dishes off to a teammate past UConn's Rudy Gay as the Tar Heels beat the University of Connecticut, 77-70. Felton had 16 points, 10 assists, and five steals. Staff Photo by Scott Lewis

Oh, there were other key factors in the victory, which secured Carolina's first 20-win season since 2000-01.

Center Sean May posted his second straight double-double with 16 points and 13 rebounds. Forward Jawad Williams, who had managed a total of just nine points in his previous three games, scored 17. Reserves Melvin Scott and Reyshawn Terry played increased minutes because illness reduced the playing time of Jackie Manuel and David Noel.

It also helped that the Huskies' leading scorer, junior Rashad Anderson, was still in the hospital getting an abscess on his right leg treated.

But it was Felton—who scored 14 of his 16 points, handed out eight of his 10 assists and committed two of his three turnovers in the second half—who pushed, pulled and prodded his team to the grinding victory.

And Felton did all that while holding Huskies point guard Marcus Williams, who had missed two days of practice with a sinus infection, to just six of his team-high 18 points after the halftime break.

"For my money," UConn coach Jim Calhoun said, "Felton is as good a point guard as I've seen. Today, he was impeccable...I thought in the first half, Marcus matched him. In the second half, Felton won the battle, certainly."

Thus, so did the Tar Heels.

Felton wasn't feeling like one of the best points guards in the country as he watched—and re-watched—film of the Duke loss with teammate May.

"He was so hurt after the game," May said. "... And we just talked about 'We're more mature now; we've got to make that play.' And Ray takes a lot of the heat on himself; and rightfully so—he's our point guard; he's our leader. We need him to feel that pain. But I said, 'Hey, that's not on you, that's on all of us.'"

That team blame was reinforced by Roy Williams at what the coach called "the best practice of the season" on Friday.

"I addressed it in front of the whole team and said, 'If you hear anybody saying anything bad about the little fella, then you better make sure you take up for him and cover him,'" said Williams, who credited Felton for leading them back from a deficit in the Duke game, but also said he would have liked his point guard to penetrate on the last play.

Still, Felton said he felt the need to prove himself after committing an uncharacteristic eight turnovers in the Duke loss—and after an ugly first half when the Tar Heels trailed 34-31 at the break.

So in the second half, with the score tied and the outcome in the balance, "I just decided to be more aggressive, to make something happen," Felton said.

And he did.

"Today, he did a great job of bouncing back," May said. "But I think [the memory of the Duke game] is still there, and I hope it is. Because down

OPPOSITE PAGE: In the first half, Jawad Williams goes to the basket past Charlie Villanueva for two of his 17 points to lead the Tar Heels past the University of Connecticut, 77-70.
Staff Photo by Scott Lewis

"Ray takes a lot of heat on himself; and rightfully so— he's our point guard; he's our leader."

—Sean May

the line, we're going to need him to remember that play to make a big play at the end of the game to win."

OPPOSITE PAGE: In the second half, UNC's Raymond Felton drives to the basket against UConn's Josh Boone as the Tar Heels beat the University of Connecticut, 77-70. Felton had 16 points, 10 assists, and five steals. Staff Photo by Scott Lewis

RIGHT: In the second half, UNC's Rashad McCants cheers on his teammates as he sits on the bench with four fouls as the Tar Heels beat the University of Connecticut, 77-70. McCants had 15 points and four rebounds. Staff Photo by Scott Lewis

	1st	2nd	Total
North Carolina	31	46	77
UConn	34	36	70

NORTH CAROLINA

Player	FGM-A	3FGM-A	FTM-A	O-D REB	A	BLK	S	TP
21 J. Williams	7-17	3-7	0-0	2-4	0	0	0	17
32 McCants	7-16	1-5	0-0	1-3	1	0	0	15
42 May	5-11	0-1	6-8	4-9	1	0	2	16
2 Felton	5-14	2-6	4-6	1-2	10	0	5	16
5 Manuel	0-1	0-0	0-0	2-0	1	0	5	0
1 Scott	0-4	0-3	0-0	0-1	1	0	1	0
3 Terry	1-1	1-1	0-0	0-0	1	1	0	3
11 Thomas	0-0	0-0	0-0	0-0	2	0	0	0
24 M. Williams	4-9	0-0	0-1	3-3	1	0	0	8
34 Noel	1-1	0-0	0-0	1-0	1	0	0	2

UCONN

Player	FGM-A	3FGM-A	FTM-A	O-D REB	A	BLK	S	TP
3 Villanueva	1-6	0-0	0-1	1-6	0	3	0	2
22 Gay	4-14	1-3	4-6	2-4	2	4	2	13
33 Brown	5-12	2-7	3-4	1-4	1	2	0	15
21 Boone	7-10	0-0	2-4	6-5	0	4	0	16
5 Williams	7-14	2-2	2-2	2-2	5	0	1	18
11 Armstrong	2-2	0-0	0-2	1-3	2	3	0	4
13 Thompson	0-0	0-0	0-0	0-0	0	0	0	0
20 Kellogg	1-4	0-2	0-0	1-5	1	0	2	2
32 Nelson	0-0	0-0	0-0	0-0	0	0	0	0

TOUGH ENOUGH

By CHIP ALEXANDER

Turns out, North Carolina didn't need Rashad McCants to beat N.C. State.

Turns out, senior Melvin Scott was more than a capable replacement. Turns out, the second-ranked Tar Heels still were too deep, too explosive, too good for the Wolfpack, even without their leading scorer.

Although the Pack could match the Heels' tenacity and hustle, with the floor burns to prove it, Carolina emerged an 81-71 winner at the RBC Center despite the absence of McCants, who missed the game with an intestinal disorder.

"It was one of those games that was tough, that wasn't pretty," UNC coach Roy Williams said. "It was difficult to play without Rashad because...he is such a threat. We said since we didn't have him, everyone else had to pick up and play well and execute offensively."

UNC point guard Raymond Felton was listening. In a near flawless performance, he had 21 points, seven assists, and no turnovers in 38 minutes. And center Sean May, working hard inside, closed with 14 points and 12 rebounds to post his fifth straight double-double.

It would be Felton and May who helped fuel a lethal offensive spurt by the Heels (23-3, 11-2) in the second half that was too much for the Wolfpack to, well, stomach.

"It separated the game," Felton said. "It kind of broke their backs."

The Pack (15-11, 5-8 ACC), needing a strong late-season run to reach the NCAA Tournament, trailed 53-50 after a three-point play by freshman forward Andrew Brackman with 10:38 left. The RBC Center was rocking, with State fans in the crowd of 19,722—many of the NCSU students with

---

OPPOSITE PAGE: In the first half UNC's Melvin Scott drills one of four three pointers during UNC's 81-71 victory at the RBC Center. Staff Photo by Ethan Hyman

painted faces and handmade signs—turning up the volume.

"We were in very good position," State's Julius Hodge said. "We needed a key stop, a key rebound, needed to hit a big shot.

"But," Hodge admitted glumly, "it didn't happen."

Instead, the Tar Heels did all of those things in finishing off a regular-season sweep of the Pack and solidifying their spot atop the ACC standings, a full game ahead of Wake Forest.

Felton missed a three-pointer from the key, but May rebounded and shot the ball back out to Felton, who never hesitated and knocked down a second try behind the arc. After a State turnover, Felton then quickly fed May for a lob dunk.

"It's the sign of a great team when they get down a little, they quickly refocus and come back strong," State forward Ilian Evtimov said. "We just couldn't stop them on defense. They knew they had to score and did what they had to do."

Moments later, UNC's Jawad Williams missed a three, but Evtimov was called for a foul on the rebound. Given a reprieve, Williams buried a three.

Hodge scored on a rebound basket, but Carolina wasn't through. Scott rushed and missed a three-point shot, but Williams gathered in the offense rebound. Felton then bombed in a three over Hodge, holding the shooter's pose for a second or two as he backpedaled down the court.

Just like that, it was 64-52, Carolina. In barely two and a half minutes, the Heels had scored 11 points

"We didn't do a good job defending the three," NCSU coach Herb Sendek said. "We made 12 but gave up 10."

With McCants out, Scott knew he had to be productive. Scott was a starter last year, but has spent his senior year coming off the bench and playing limited minutes.

"I decided to start Melvin because he is the most experienced one to start a game on the road," Roy Williams said. "Melvin is usually the first guy to come in for Rashad, so it made sense. I also thought it was important for us to have a guy who could make shots."

Scott knocked in a three on his first shot of the game. He also ended the first half with a three from the left corner just before the buzzer, giving the Heels a 38-33 halftime lead.

"I told him before the game, 'Just play like you've always played in your career,'" May said.

Scott had scored 36 points in his last 10 games, going 6-for-24 on threes. But he had 12 points against the Pack, hitting four of eight shots from three-point range.

"It was great, man, to get the opportunity to play," Scott said. "I know what I can do. It was a matter of stepping up when they needed me."

Hodge, trying too hard to be too good, pressing in the first half, had 20 points for the Pack but also five of State's 13 turnovers. State was 12-of-27 on threes, but the Heels were quick to the ball and usually contested the shots.

OPPOSITE PAGE: UNC's Joe Holladay, left, and Roy Williams yell at the officials in the second half of the Tar Heels' 81-71 win over N.C. State. Staff Photo by Scott Lewis

"It separated the game. It kinda broke their backs."

—Raymond Felton

"We knew the only thing they could kill us with would be the three," May said. "We made them take tough shots."

"We just want to keep playing, keep it going," Felton said. "Hopefully we'll be the ACC champion at the end of the season."

	1st	2nd	Total
North Carolina	38	43	81
N.C. State	33	38	71

NORTH CAROLINA

Player	FGM-A	3FGM-A	FTM-A	O-D REB	A	BLK	S	TP
1 Scott	4-8	4-8	0-0	1-1	3	1	0	12
2 Felton	6-13	2-6	7-9	0-5	7	0	1	21
5 Manuel	1-2	0-0	0-0	1-1	0	0	0	2
21 J. Williams	5-10	3-5	2-2	3-3	3	0	1	15
42 May	7-14	0-0	0-0	4-8	2	0	0	14
0 Holley	0-0	0-0	0-0	0-0	0	0	0	0
3 Terry	1-3	1-1	0-0	1-1	0	2	0	3
11 Thomas	0-0	0-0	0-0	0-0	0	0	0	0
22 Miller	0-0	0-0	0-0	0-0	0	0	0	0
24 M. Williams	2-3	0-1	10-12	0-2	1	0	3	14
34 Noel	0-0	0-0	0-0	0-0	1	0	0	0
35 Hooker	0-0	0-0	0-0	0-0	0	0	0	0
41 Sanders	0-0	0-0	0-0	0-0	0	0	0	0

N.C. STATE

Player	FGM-A	3FGM-A	FTM-A	O-D REB	A	BLK	S	TP
3 Evtimov	1-2	1-2	0-0	0-4	0	0	2	3
14 Atsur	4-13	2-8	4-4	2-2	3	0	1	14
22 Bethel	2-6	2-5	0-0	1-2	2	0	1	6
20 Hodge	7-16	4-5	2-2	1-3	5	0	1	20
32 Collins	5-9	1-3	2-2	1-0	2	0	0	13
11 Grant	0-1	0-1	0-0	0-0	1	0	0	0
13 Bennerman	1-2	1-2	2-2	1-0	0	0	0	5
33 Simmons	1-1	0-0	0-1	0-4	1	4	0	2
40 Brackman	3-3	1-1	1-1	0-0	0	0	0	8

OPPOSITE PAGE: State's Julius Hodge can only watch as UNC's Jawad Williams slams home a second-half dunk in the RBC Center in Raleigh, NC. UNC held off the Pack to won the game. Staff Photo by Chuck Liddy

BELOW: In the second half, UNC's Raymond Felton is fouled by N.C. State's Cedric Simmons as he drives to the basket past State's Andrew Brackman as the Tar Heels win 81-71. Staff Photo by Scott Lewis

#42 SEAN MAY

By Keith Parsons *Associated Press*

Sean May loves pizza and cookies almost as much as double-doubles. Unfortunately, he couldn't have a lot of all three.

So the 6-foot-9 center for North Carolina decided to alter his lifestyle, beginning with what he ate. The fattening foods were out, replaced by lots of grilled chicken and other healthy stuff.

"My trainer, he calls me the cookie monster because he knows how much I love cookies, so I try to stay away from it," May said Thursday. "I tried to eat as healthy as I could to stay fresh and to not put on the extra pounds."

The willpower—and all the extra work on his conditioning—certainly paid off. May is averaging career highs in points (16.8) and rebounds (10.8) as a junior while being named second-team All-America. More importantly, he's a big reason the Tar Heels earned a No. 1 seed in the NCAA tournament.

May lost about 15 pounds in the off-season to get down to about 250, so he's still burly enough to be a dominant presence in the paint. Down the stretch, while North Carolina (29-4) was wrapping up its first outright Atlantic Coast Conference regular-season title since 1993, May strung together eight consecutive double-doubles.

The run was capped by a brilliant individual effort against Duke: 26 points and 24 rebounds. No wonder Villanova coach Jay Wright called May the best post player in college basketball.

"I think he's got the whole package, so you're going to have to guard him on the perimeter, run the floor with him, guard him in the post," Wright said. "Can't be many more problems than that."

This kind of season is exactly why May spurned his hometown school of Indiana to come to North Carolina. His father, Scott, led the Hoosiers to the 1976 national title, and fans all around the state fully expected Sean to do the same.

"I always loved Indiana basketball. I grew up watching it, but this is home for me and it worked out great for me now," May said. "It was tough on my family and my father, who played there. He did so much for that university and cares so much about that university.

"But I'm happy to be here. I bleed Carolina blue."

Tar Heels coach Roy Williams is more than pleased to have May, particularly the slimmed-down version.

"I think he's really made some significant strides, and probably, in the off-season, worked as hard as any guy that I have ever had working on his body," Williams said. "I think that his success is directly related to that hard work that he put in."

And May is proud of the legacy he already has at North Carolina. He and his teammates have led a complete turnaround from the 8-20 record of three seasons ago.

Helping Williams win his first national championship completes the rebuilding.

"I think about it all the time," May said. "Being able to walk over in St. Louis and give him a hug and be one of the first players to bring home his national championship."

Name: Sean May
Born: April 4, 1984
Hometown: Bloomington, Indiana
Attended: Bloomington North (IN)
Position: Forward / Center
Height: 6 foot 9
Weight: 250 pounds

A FORTUNATE HORN

By ROBBI PICKERAL

As North Carolina center Sean May celebrated his game-saving block—perhaps, he sheepishly admitted later, a second or two too early—all teammate Jackie Manuel could think was, "Get the ball! Get the ball!"

It was only when Manuel grabbed the loose sphere, held on to his career-high 10th rebound and heard the final horn sound at Comcast Center that the slippery senior finally could enjoy the significance of the second-ranked Heels' 85-83 victory at Maryland:

A record of 6-2 on the road against ACC foes for the first time since 2000-01; and a winning mark in that category for the first time in his career.

"We've come a long way," said Manuel, whose team was a combined 4-20 on the road against league foes the previous three seasons. "Last year, we struggled on the road. We had a lot of problems on the road winning close games. This year, we've

matured so much. Guys feed off each other; we work together. Even when we're down, we know we're not out."

That was certainly the case in the final minute as the Terps (16-10, 7-8 ACC) whittled an 11-point second-half deficit and tied it 83-83 with 41.5 seconds left on a putback by Ekene Ibekwe.

Before the game, UNC (24-3, 12-2) coach Roy Williams had reminded his players that two characteristics are key to winning on the road: Poise and toughness.

In the final minute, point guard Raymond Felton epitomized poise.

May symbolized the toughness.

With 18.9 seconds left and the crowd on its feet, screeching and preaching defense, Felton calmly

---

OPPOSTIE PAGE: In the second half, UNC's Sean May dunks on Maryland's Nik Caner-Medley as the Tar Heels win 85-83. May led the Heels with 22 points and 11 rebounds.
Staff Photo by Scott Lewis

drove past John Gilchrist—with help from a Jawad Williams pick—to score the go-ahead layup.

"John got hit on the screen, and I saw an open lane to the basket, and I took it," said the modest Felton, who notched the 12th double-double of his college career (10 points, 10 assists).

UNC slapped the ball out of bounds under Maryland's basket, and Gilchrist inbounded it to Mike Jones with 6.9 seconds left. But as Jones drove to the basket, Manuel defending on his hip, May stepped up, jumped out and cleanly blocked the shot.

Jones said he never saw May coming.

"All I could think was, 'Don't let him get a shot off,'" said an excited May, who finished with three blocks but also a sixth consecutive double-double (22 points, 11 rebounds).

The last Tar Heels player to record six in a row was Antawn Jamison at the end of the 1997-98 season.

May said he knew he—and his teammates— had to intensify their play to win a second road game without leading scorer Rashad McCants, who missed his second consecutive contest with an intestinal disorder.

So they did. In addition to Manuel's, Felton's, and May's marks, David Noel scored a season-high 12 points and Jawad Williams chipped in 21. Senior Melvin Scott, starting in place of McCants, played 27 minutes.

"Even when we're down, we know we're not out."

—Jackie Manuel

Lesser used guys also contributed. Back-up point guard Quentin Thomas made his ninth field goal of the year and reserve swingman Reyshawn Terry contributed his sixth and seventh assists of the season.

UNC solidified the 40th time in 52 ACC seasons that it has finished .500 or better on the road against conference teams. It also stayed a half-game ahead of Wake Forest atop the ACC standings.

"It was a heck of a college basketball game," Roy Williams said. "And needless to say, we feel very fortunate."

No wonder, as Manuel held the ball in his hands as the final seconds ticked off the clock, he smiled.

"I knew there was still time left," Manuel said. "I was glad to hear that horn."

OPPOSITE PAGE: In the second half, UNC's Raymond Felton splits the defense of Maryland's James Gist, left, and Ekene Ibekwe as the Tar Heels win 85-83. Felton had 10 points, 10 assists, and two steals. Staff Photo by Scott Lewis

ABOVE: UNC's David Noel chases down a loose ball tailed by Maryland's Mike Jones as the Tar Heels win 85-83. Noel had 12 points, three assists, and two steals. Staff Photo by Scott Lewis

LEFT: In the second half, UNC's Jackie Manuel brings one of his three steals up-court past Maryland's John Gilchrist as the Tar Heels win 85-83. Manuel had nine points and 10 rebounds. Staff Photo by Scott Lewis

OPPOSITE PAGE: In the first half, UNC's Jackie Manuel pressures Maryland's Mike Jones as Jones falls during the Tar Heels 85-83 win. Staff Photo by Scott Lewis

"I was glad to hear that horn."

—Jackie Manuel

	1st	2nd	Total
North Carolina	47	38	85
Maryland	37	46	83

NORTH CAROLINA

Player	FGM-A	3FGM-A	FTM-A	O-D REB	A	BLK	S	TP
5 Manuel	4-8	1-2	0-2	5-5	2	1	3	9
21 J. Williams	7-11	3-6	4-5	0-4	1	0	0	21
42 May	8-16	0-0	6-8	5-6	0	3	0	22
1 Scott	1-5	1-4	0-0	0-0	0	0	0	3
2 Felton	4-11	2-6	0-0	2-2	10	0	2	10
3 Terry	0-0	0-0	1-2	0-1	2	0	0	1
11 Thomas	1-1	0-0	0-0	0-0	0	0	0	2
24 M. Williams	1-3	0-1	3-4	0-5	0	1	1	5
34 Noel	5-7	2-3	0-0	0-4	3	1	2	12

MARYLAND

Player	FGM-A	3FGM-A	FTM-A	O-D REB	A	BLK	S	TP
21 Grinnon	0-1	0-0	0-0	0-1	0	0	0	0
22 Caner-Medley	7-18	1-3	1-1	0-5	0	1	0	16
4 Garrison	0-5	0-0	1-2	2-1	0	3	1	1
11 Gilchrist	4-9	1-3	4-4	1-1	5	0	0	13
13 McCray	7-12	5-6	6-6	3-3	5	0	1	25
12 Ledbetter	1-1	0-0	0-0	0-0	2	0	1	2
15 Gist	4-8	0-0	0-0	2-5	1	0	1	8
23 Jones	4-8	4-5	0-0	1-3	1	1	0	12
25 Ibekwe	2-6	0-0	0-0	3-0	0	0	0	4
31 Bowers	1-3	0-0	0-0	1-0	0	1	0	2

#2 RAYMOND FELTON

By Robbi Pickeral

During the early weeks of his thrice-a-day workouts last summer, North Carolina point guard Raymond Felton occasionally grew tired.

Tired of hearing his dad remind him to pull his right elbow in. Tired of hearing his conscience tell him to straighten his arm. Tired of hearing the ball go "clank" instead of "swish."

But the fleet-footed, hard-headed junior always returned to mastering new mechanics during his 600-jump-shots-a-day regimen, because he was frankly more tired of something else: hearing opponents, NBA analysts, and even fans say he couldn't shoot.

"He could dribble, he could pass, he could do all these things," said his father, Raymond Felton Sr. "But when it came to shooting, people would go, 'Well, he doesn't have a consistent shot.' I think hearing that finally got to him ...What he was doing wasn't working, so he had to try something new."

"Something new" meant tucking his shooting elbow closer to his body and turning what coach Roy Williams called a "technically wrong" chicken-wing-like form into a more vertical motion.

As a result, Felton now releases the ball from a more consistent spot to the right of his head instead of pushing it across the front of his face and shooting it off target.

With the change, he made 52.6 percent of his shots overall and 55 percent of his three-point attempts, up from 42 percent and 31.2 percent, respectively, last season. Felton, who said he's shooting better than he ever has, even converted 12 three-pointers in a row during an early stretch of the season.

"He's got his elbow in tighter; it's not flying like it was last year. He's not shooting the ball across his face like it was last year," Williams said. "I feel that by the end of the season, his numbers shooting the basketball will be a lot better than they were last year."

However, whether he'll stay that accurate remains to be seen. It's not easy for a player to change his shooting mechanics after high school, coaches caution. Felton is trying to overcome habits that have been part of his natural routine since he first picked up a basketball more than a dozen years ago.

Imagine a surgeon having to hold a scalpel differently than she usually does, or a novelist finding the letters on his keyboard in different places. Now imagine them having to master those changes in three months.

"A guy that gets into college, if he has some mechanical flaws, by this time they're such habits that it's very difficult to change," Williams said. "You can help someone, you can improve someone, but you're not going to take a guy who has got a terrible shot and make him into a pure shooter unless he's an unusual situation."

One of the most unusual Williams has seen was the improvement of Kirk Hinrich at Kansas. As a freshman, the guard shot 31.3 percent from three-point range. By his sophomore season, he was shooting 50.5 percent.

Hinrich, however, did nothing technically wrong on his shot; he just had to practice it more, Williams said.

The same was true, Wake Forest coach Skip Prosser said, of former Wake star Josh Howard and a former Xavier player named Lenny Brown.

Still, such examples are so rare that N.C. State coach Herb Sendek couldn't think of a player he has coached who dramatically improved his shot during his college career.

"No one just pops to mind," Sendek said. "I think most of the guys we've had probably fall into that overwhelming majority where they were either pretty good shooters and still made shots, or they were guys who might have marginally improved but didn't go from Dennis Rodman to Steve Kerr."

Felton's shooting was never so bad that it could be described as Rodman-esque. As a high school player, he broke the South Carolina career scoring record with 2,992 points and averaged 30.8 points his senior season. As a freshman and sophomore at Carolina, he made 40.7 percent of his shots and averaged 12.2 points.

But one reason he scored so many points in high school, his dad noted, was the 20 to 25 shots he took per game. He could afford to miss a few at the beginning and

Name: Raymond Felton
Born: June 26, 1984
Hometown: Latta, South Carolina
Attended: Latta High School (SC)
Position: Guard
Height: 6 foot 1
Weight: 198 pounds

Staff Photo by Scott Lewis

have time to find his rhythm by the end. In Williams's system this season, he's averaging only 6.5 shots.

"I have to make the most of every opportunity," he said. So far, he has.

"I think he's finally transforming people's perceptions to 'hey, this kid can play,'" center Sean May said. "We know he can do everything with the ball, we know he understands the game, we know he can make the incredible play. But just being able to knock down that 19-, 20-footer—25 feet when he gets to the NBA—it's going to be huge for him. It's going to get huge for his future."

Felton actually tried to bring in his elbow and transform his shooting as a freshman at the suggestion of then-coach Matt Doherty. Doherty pointed out then, Felton Sr. said, that a change in shooting technique could help his son's NBA prospects.

But by the end of December 2002, he was shooting 35.7 percent from the field and 25 percent from three-point range. "I just didn't feel comfortable with it, so I went back," Felton said.

"I don't know that he believed in it that much," Felton Sr. said.

His son loved Doherty, he added, "but back then, he was coming off [starring] in high school, player of the year, all that. He didn't think he needed to change."

Felton said he changed his mind again over the the summer so he could make himself a better player and better help the Tar Heels.

And that's why Felton went to the gym three times a day last summer, tucking in his elbow as he worked on three-pointers, running shots, 14-footers, everything.

"It's natural now," Felton said of his new motion. "... Just working, working, working, it finally came naturally."

Swingman Rashad McCants, arguably the team's best outside shooter, was working out with Felton and former UNC point guard Shammond Williams over the summer when McCants realized that Felton was swishing more shots than he was.

"I watched him shoot, and he was just flipping his wrist real hard and it just really looked perfect," McCants said. "And I just told him, 'I think I need to start shooting like you, flipping my wrist as hard and getting more spin.'"

So McCants changed his shot, too.

"I think it paid off," he said.

MAY'S MIGHTY NIGHT

By ROBBI PICKERAL

With North Carolina trailing at home at halftime for the first time this season, ailing swingman Rashad McCants pulled center Sean May aside and gave him these instructions:

"Quietly take over this game."

May complied with the "take over" part by scoring 23 second-half points in the second-ranked Tar Heels' 91-76 basketball victory over Florida State.

It was the "quietly" part he just couldn't manage while helping UNC clinch a share of the ACC regular-season title for the first time since 2001.

"Thirty-two and 12 speaks for itself," coach Roy Williams said after the game, referring to his big man's stats.

Not quite.

—May's 32 points were a career high and the most any Heels player has scored since Joseph Forte notched 36 against FSU in 2001.

—His 12 rebounds marked his seventh straight double-double, the most since Mitch Kupchak posted eight in a row in 1975-76.

—He also became the 57th UNC player to score 1,000 points. Teammates McCants, Jawad Williams and Raymond Felton already have reached that plateau, marking only the second time in the program's history that there are four 1,000-point scorers on the same team.

—Now averaging 16.3 points and 10.4 rebounds, May stayed on pace to become the 13th UNC player to average a double-double.

OPPOSITE PAGE: In the second half, Sean May dunks for two of his career high 32 points as the Tar Heels beat Florida State, 91-76. May also had 12 rebounds. Staff Photo by Scott Lewis

"We've come a long way, but we're not done," said May, who also contributed a blocked shot and a steal. "We want to win it outright."

With McCants watching from the bench in street clothes—he missed his third straight game because of an intestinal disorder—UNC was downright sloppy at times in the first half and allowed feisty FSU to shoot 60 percent before halftime.

Trailing by three points after the Seminoles ended the first period with an 11-0 run, May said Williams told his team, "If you want to do what we talked about at the beginning of the season and hang up banners and be what people call a championship team, you've got to do the things that got you here."

"So we had to turn it up a notch," May said.

Carolina trailed 54-52 with about 13 minutes left but finally pulled away with a 15-2 tear that included three straight field goals from May. That resulted in a 67-56 lead, UNC's largest to that point in the game.

The Heels didn't build much on that lead, but May finally picked up his 10th rebound with 3:23 left when he grabbed the ball off a missed free throw by FSU's Al Thornton.

"I didn't know [my numbers until] we went out of the TV timeout with about 3:20 or something left," May said. "And I looked up; I wasn't sure how many points I had, but I knew I had nine rebounds.

"They were shooting a free throw, and I just told myself, 'If this comes off of the rim, I've got it. Nobody's getting this ball.'"

Once he grabbed it, passed it, and popped up from tumbling to the floor, he threw down a dunk to tie his career high of 28 points.

"He was phenomenal," said David Noel, who had a career-high eight assists. "It was one of the best performances I've ever seen. I think he got me seven of my assists, so I appreciate that."

In addition, point guard Raymond Felton recorded his sixth double-double of the season with 15 points and 10 assists. Freshman Marvin Williams, whose sprained toe was feeling worse than usual before the game, coach Roy Williams said, chipped in 17 points.

Thornton led FSU with 19 points. But teammate Adam Waleskowski, who had 13 points in the first half, failed to score in the second half as the Seminoles shot 36.7 percent.

UNC, meanwhile, shot a sizzling 62.1 percent after the break, led by May's 10-for-10 effort.

"Raymond, David, and Jackie [Manuel] were doing a great job of driving and penetrating, and Marvin stepped out and hit some shots, so things opened up inside for me," May said. "It was the easiest [32] points I've ever had in terms of, all I had to do was catch the ball and lay it right in.

"I wasn't making too many shots over people, and I don't think I even had to use a post move tonight. The guards did a great job of driving and finding me for open looks."

ABOVE: UNC's Sean May celebrates with Raymond Felton after a dunk that put UNC up by nine in the first half.
Staff Photo by Lisa Lauck

	1st	2nd	Total
Florida State	44	32	76
North Carolina	41	50	91

FLORIDA STATE

Player	FGM-A	3FGM-A	FTM-A	O-D REB	A	BLK	S	TP
4 Galloway	3-5	1-2	0-0	0-3	6	0	4	7
12 Thornton	8-10	1-1	2-4	1-5	0	1	1	19
32 Johnson	2-2	0-0	2-2	1-0	0	0	0	6
22 Wafer	0-1	0-1	0-0	0-1	0	0	0	0
21 Rich	4-11	0-0	0-0	0-3	2	0	1	8
51 Waleskowski	5-10	3-4	0-0	3-2	4	0	1	13
3 Swann	4-12	3-8	0-0	1-2	2	0	3	11
10 Mims	0-1	0-0	2-2	0-0	1	0	0	2
20 Wilson	1-5	1-4	0-0	0-0	3	0	0	3
54 Richardson	2-3	1-1	2-2	1-1	2	0	0	7
25 Romero	0-0	0-0	0-0	0-0	0	0	0	0

NORTH CAROLINA

Player	FGM-A	3FGM-A	FTM-A	O-D REB	A	BLK	S	TP
21 J. Williams	3-7	1-3	0-0	0-2	0	0	0	7
42 May	13-15	0-0	6-10	3-9	0	1	1	32
5 Manuel	2-4	0-0	4-4	2-0	1	1	0	8
1 Scott	2-6	2-6	0-0	1-1	3	0	1	6
2 Felton	4-10	1-3	6-7	0-5	10	0	4	15
24 M. Williams	7-11	2-3	1-2	0-4	1	0	1	17
34 Noel	2-5	0-1	0-0	1-2	8	0	2	4
11 Thomas	1-1	0-0	0-0	0-1	0	0	1	2
3 Terry	0-0	0-0	0-0	0-0	0	0	1	0

"We've come a long way, but we're not done."

—Sean May

ABOVE: In the second half, Marvin Williams shoots for two over FSU's Anthony Richardson as the Tar Heels beat Florida State, 91-76. Williams had 17 points and four rebounds. Staff Photo by Scott Lewis

#24 MARVIN WILLIAMS

By Robbi Pickeral

If you like the way freshman Marvin Williams moves his feet on defense, boxes out for rebounds and follows through on his plethora of shots, credit former North Carolina coach Dean Smith.

At least partially.

Williams, the 6-foot-9 McDonald's All-American who has averaged 8.3 points and four rebounds off the bench in his first four games, grew up watching an old set of Smith's instructional videos owned by his father, Marvin Williams Sr.

That fueled the teenager's love of Carolina, and his versatility as a player.

"Marvin, he's something special," said UNC center Sean May. "He's so quick...that he can do a lot of different things out there. Which means we as a team can do a lot of different things out there."

Indeed, Williams—a jack-in-the-box jumper who runs the court with the grace of a ghost and battles like a prize fighter for rebounds—can play any of the three frontcourt positions. However, he is still developing facets of each.

"He can slide his feet well enough to guard somebody out on the floor," coach Roy Williams said, meaning he has the ability defend small forwards. That's an intimidating prospect for all of those 6-4 and 6-5 wings in the ACC.

However, "he's not had any time as an offensive 3-man, and right now is not ready to do that," Coach Williams added.

So when the Tar Heels practice with three of their biggest guys—6-9 May, 6-9 Marvin Williams, and 6-9 Jawad Williams—on the floor, Marvin has been playing small forward on defense and power forward on offense. Jawad, the opposite.

The lineup hasn't been seen much in games yet, but it has great potential.

Just like Marvin Williams.

"I just want to be the very best player I can be," said Marvin, adding that his favorite shot is "anything that scores" and his favorite position is "whatever Coach Williams tells me to play."

The learning and social aspects of college, he said, are why he chose to come to Carolina instead of heading straight for the NBA out of Bremerton (Washington) High.

"I wanted to be a kid for a little bit longer, you know?" Marvin asked quietly, looking the question-asker in the eye. "I just didn't feel like I was ready for the NBA yet. I wanted to experience college basketball."

The former Homecoming King and junior-year soccer goalie says it all with refreshing humility and honesty—the same way he still calls everyone "sir" and "ma'am" and even smiles a bit during freshman duties such as carrying bags.

"The thing I love best about Marvin is he's a better person than a basketball player," said his high school coach, Casey Lindberg.

Which says a lot, because he's awful good on the basketball court.

Marvin Williams, who has also studied tapes of "Pistol" Pete Maravich and whose favorite NBA player is Kevin Garnett, worked hard on diversifying his game through high school. He always carried a basketball from class to class, dribbling in-between to practice his ballhandling skills. He also liked to take the toughest defensive assignments during games—no matter the size of his opponent.

"He could get out and sit in that defensive position, and he could stop people 20 feet from the basket as easily as he could in the post," Lindberg said. "He really loved that challenge."

Marvin said the toughest adjustment from high school to college is the intensity level, but he credits his teammates and coaches for their patience and help.

Name: Marvin Williams
Born: June 19, 1986
Hometown: Bremerton, Washington
Attended: Bremerton High School (WA)
Position: Forward
Height: 6 foot 9
Weight: 230 pounds

Staff Photo by Scott Lewis

As for NBA—the place where Marvin ultimately does want to go—Williams said he's not thinking about it, at least not yet.

There is plenty of conjecture among fans that he might leave after one or two seasons if UNC is successful. But Marvin said: "Only God knows. Hopefully, I'll be in college all four years, and we'll see what happens from there. But if I was fortunate enough to be able to leave early, that would be nice, too. Right now, I just want to go to school and enjoy college basketball."

Which includes improving upon all of those things he first studied on Coach Smith's tapes. So that he can improve his versatility, as well as his team's.

"He's trying to make plays; he's not been nearly as successful as he's going to be, but he hasn't let that dampen his enthusiasm," Roy Williams said."...With experience, and learning what's going on in college basketball, he's going to be much more effective."

THE RETURN TO NO. 1

By ROBBI PICKERAL

So this is what it is supposed to mean to be a North Carolina basketball player—the lone No. 1 finisher in the ACC regular season for the first time since 1993, the No. 1 seed in the upcoming league tournament for the first time since that same season.

And after topping archrival Duke 75-73 on a late-game three-point play that emptied the stands and saw the Smith Center nets snipped down—possibly a No. 1 ranking in The Associated Press poll for the first time since 2001.

"This feeling I have...I've never felt it before," said red-eyed senior Jackie Manuel, one of three holdovers from the 8-20 team in 2001-02.

Neither had any other current Tar Heels player.

That is, until junior David Noel popped the ball out of Duke point guard Daniel Ewing's hands from behind with 27.8 seconds left, and teammate Raymond Felton jumped on it at midcourt and signalled a timeout to give UNC one last chance.

Until Felton got fouled eight seconds later, missed his second free throw, and tipped the rebound to teammate Marvin Williams—who scored a layup and got fouled for a three-point play to give UNC a two-point lead with 17 seconds left.

Then Duke supershooter J.J. Redick, who was held scoreless in the second half, missed a potential winning three-pointer from the left wing. Ewing grabbed the ball and followed with a missed 15-footer, but UNC center Sean May came down with his career-high 24th rebound to seal the frenetic final minute.

OPPOSITE PAGE: Lifted by his teammates, UNC's Raymond Felton celebrates the Tar Heels 75-73 win over Duke. Felton had 11 points, six assists, and two steals.
Staff Photo by Scott Lewis

"It was a heck of a finish," said UNC coach Roy Williams, whose team improved to 26-3 overall, 14-2 in the ACC and has won seven in a row.

"But," cautioned UNC senior Jawad Williams, "it's not over yet."

Indeed, No. 6 Duke (22-5, 11-5 ACC) has the third seed in the ACC Tournament, meaning another classic rematch could be in the works if each team wins its next two games. Both have first-round byes, and will play separately in the quarter-finals on Friday.

But of the loss, Duke forward Shavlik Randolph said, "It'll linger a bit."

For both teams, in opposite emotional ways.

Duke was playing its third straight game without starting guard Sean Dockery, who is out for the season. But even though the thin Blue Devils got into foul trouble early, when Randolph picked up his third with 11:31 left in the first half, they built as much as a nine-point lead with 3:07 left in regulation.

A five-minute UNC scoring drought early in the second half helped, as did 15 second-half points from junior Lee Melchionni and five second-half blocks from center Shelden Williams (22 points).

"You have to give credit to Carolina," Melchionni said, "but we felt like this game was ours."

And it would have been, too, Ewing said, if not for Marvin Williams's clutch grab and three-point play.

"I thought it could have been an over-the-back call on him," said Ewing, who had 11 points and nine assists but took responsibility for the loss because of his late turnovers.

"It was a loose ball situation, and he came up with it. That was a big play right there. If we get that rebound, despite what had happened, we probably would have won that game."

UNC senior Melvin Scott, who was wearing a newly cut Smith Center net around his neck, agreed, and planned to thank the freshman forward over and over again.

"What a big-time play," Scott said. "I might have to take Marvin to the mall tomorrow and buy him something."

Despite Carolina's late heroics, Blue Devils coach Mike Krzyzewski said he was proud of his team's performance and credited Carolina—particularly May, who he called "fantastic."

How good is Carolina? That, too, remained to be seen.

After the game, UNC fans were already acting as if they have the top team in the nation, rushing the floor so quickly that Roy Williams had to grab a microphone and ask them to go back to their seats so the seniors could give their Senior Day speeches.

Manuel, Scott, and Jawad Williams, however, enjoyed the victory, the crowd and the moment so much that none could hold back tears. Neither could their teammates and coaches.

Then again, that's what's part of being a winning Carolina basketball player, as well.

"We have a lot more to do, a lot more games to play," Manuel said. "But I will never, ever forget this...and how far we have come."

ABOVE: In the first half, UNC's Raymond Felton drives the lane into pressure by Duke's Shelden Williams as the Tar Heels win 75-73. Felton had 11 points, six assists, and two steals. Staff Photo by Scott Lewis

"This feeling I have...I've never felt it before."

—Jackie Manuel

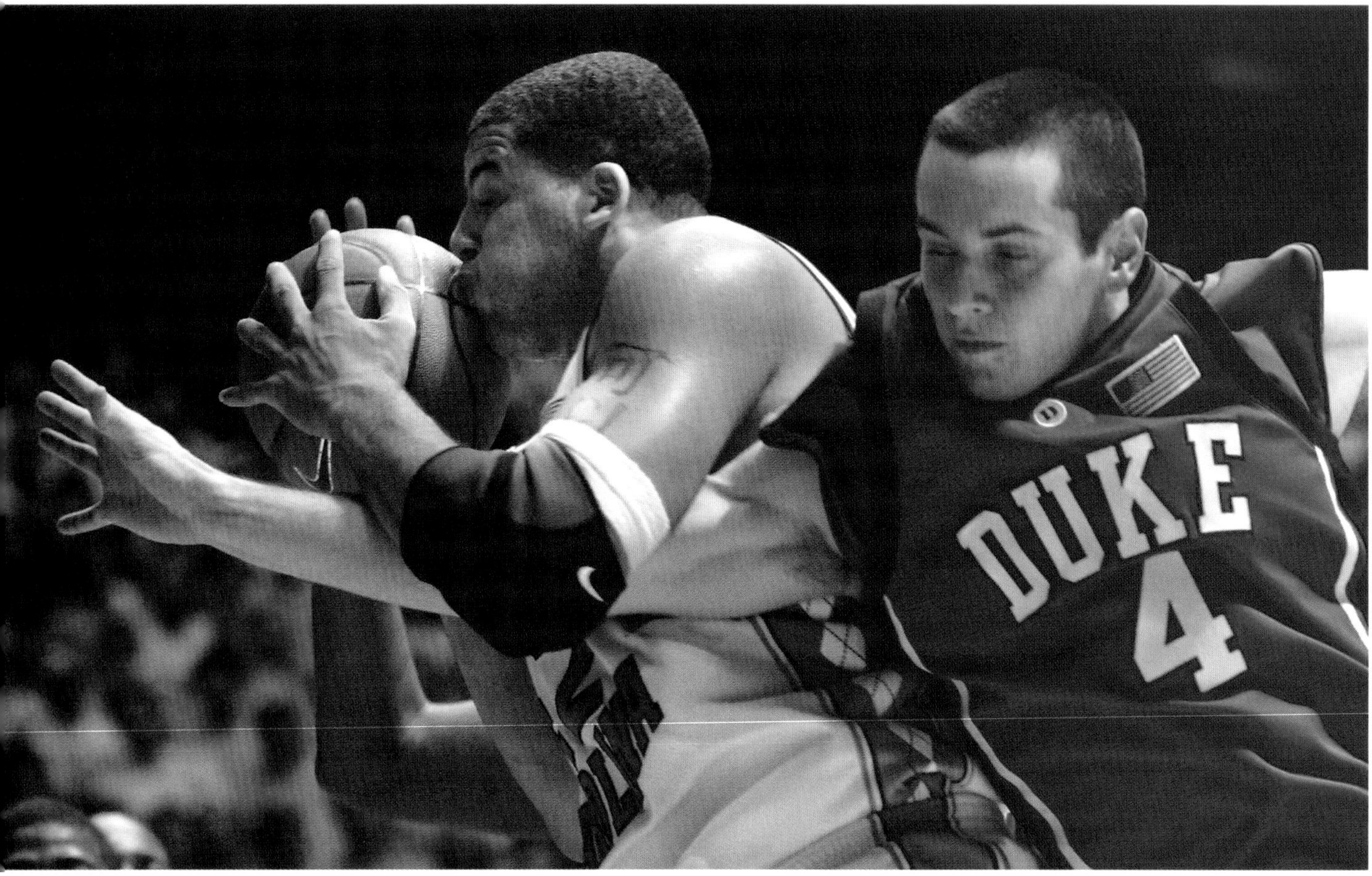
DUKE
4

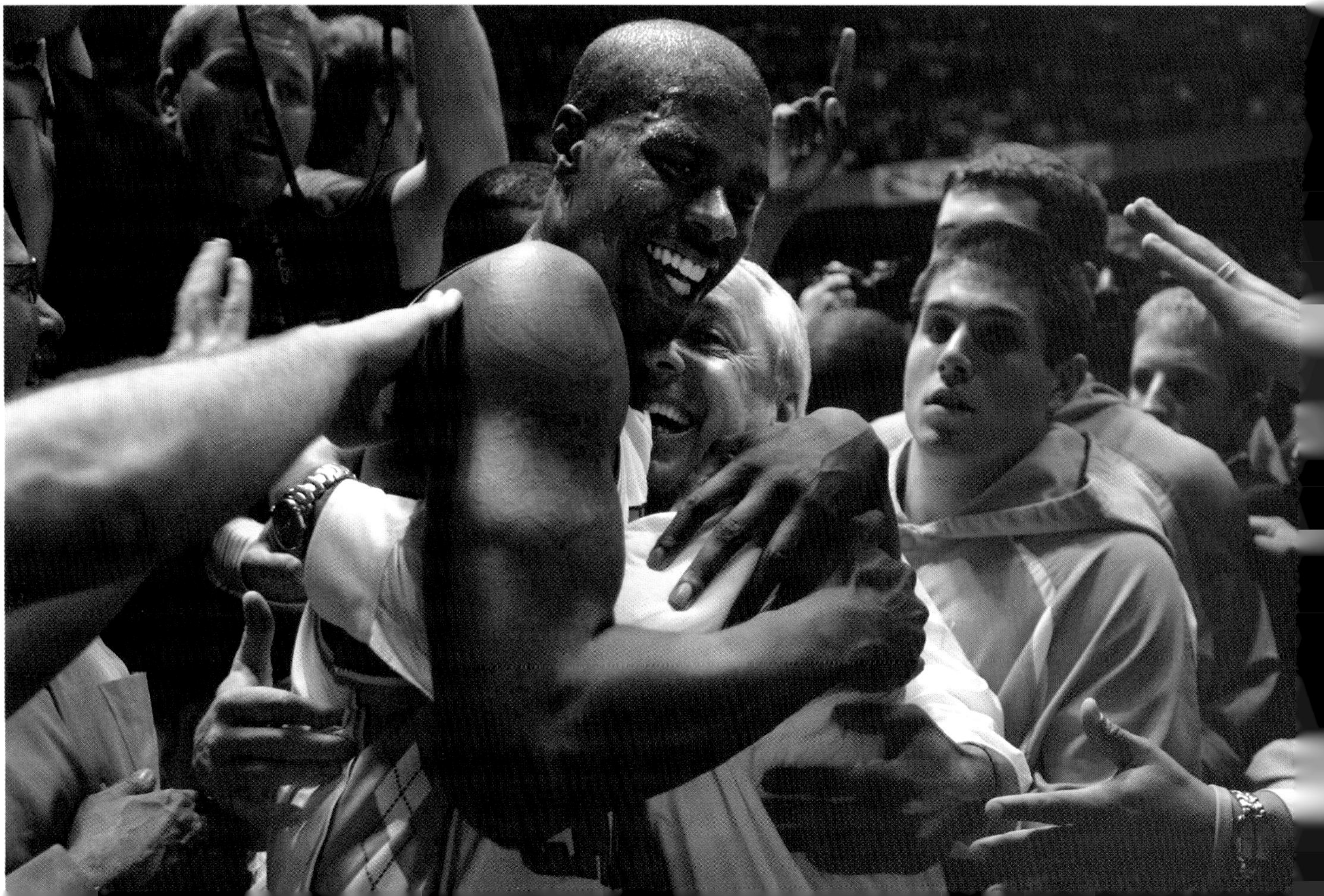

OPPOSITE PAGE TOP: UNC's Sean May grabs one of his 24 rebounds as J.J. Redick gets tangled in May's arms as the Tar Heels win 75-73. May was the game's high scorer with 26. Staff Photo by Scott Lewis

OPPOSITE PAGE BOTTOM: UNC's Marvin Williams celebrates the Tar Heels' 75-73 win over Duke with head coach Roy Williams. Marvin made the winning basket and drew a foul to seal the win. Staff Photo by Scott Lewis

BELOW: UNC's Melvin Scott walks off the court with one of the two nets over his head after the Tar Heels' beat Duke 75-73. Scott, a senior, had three rebounds, one assist, one block, and one steal. Staff Photo by Scott Lewis

	1st	2nd	Total
Duke	41	32	73
North Carolina	47	28	75

DUKE

Player	FGM-A	3FGM-A	FTM-A	O-D REB	A	BLK	S	TP
13 Melchionni	5-13	5-11	0-0	1-4	0	0	0	15
42 Randolph	1-3	0-1	1-2	0-3	1	1	0	3
23 Williams	10-13	0-0	2-5	1-3	0	6	4	22
4 Redick	5-13	4-9	3-4	0-2	6	0	0	17
5 Ewing	4-10	2-7	1-2	1-2	9	0	2	11
30 Love	0-1	0-0	0-0	0-0	1	0	0	0
21 Nelson	1-3	0-1	1-3	3-4	0	0	0	3
14 McClure	0-0	0-0	2-3	0-0	0	0	0	2
51 Johnson	0-0	0-0	0-0	1-0	0	0	0	0
41 Davidson	0-0	0-0	0-0	0-0	0	0	0	0
40 Perkins	0-0	0-0	0-0	0-0	0	0	0	0

NORTH CAROLINA

Player	FGM-A	3FGM-A	FTM-A	O-D REB	A	BLK	S	TP
21 J. Williams	3-10	0-3	2-2	2-1	0	0	0	8
35 Hooker	0-0	0-0	0-0	0-0	0	0	0	0
15 Everett	0-0	0-0	0-0	0-0	0	0	0	0
5 Manuel	5-6	0-0	2-4	0-1	2	1	1	12
1 Scott	0-2	0-2	0-0	0-3	1	1	1	0
2 Felton	3-13	0-3	5-8	1-2	6	0	2	11
42 May	10-19	0-0	6-7	12-12	3	0	2	26
24 M. Williams	3-9	0-1	3-3	2-5	0	1	0	9
34 Noel	2-4	0-1	0-0	0-1	2	0	2	4
3 Terry	1-4	1-1	2-2	2-0	0	0	0	5
11 Thomas	0-0	0-0	0-0	0-0	0	0	0	0

ATLANTIC COAST CONFERENCE

RIGHT: UNC's Rashad McCants sits alone at center court, taking in the moment, after his team headed for the locker room before their game against Clemson University in a second-round game in The ACC Tournament. It was McCants's first game back after an intestinal disorder sidelined him for the past four games. Staff Photo by Corey Lowenstein

ESCAPING THE TIGERS

By Robbi Pickeral

North Carolina swingman Rashad McCants saw the loose ball near midcourt with 6:52 left, and all he could think was, "Get it."

Yes, he had missed four straight games with an intestinal disorder. Sure, he was six pounds lighter and had gone through only two full practices in the past two weeks. But "I never felt like my talent had disappeared or anything," the junior said after top-seeded UNC overcame a 13-point, second-half deficit to beat ninth-seeded Clemson 88-81 in the quarterfinals of the ACC Tournament.

And when he dove on the ball, out-grappling Tigers guard Cliff Hammonds to force a change of possession and solidify a change of momentum, McCants proved it in front of a sellout crowd at MCI Center.

"It was good of him to sacrifice his body like that...considering everything he's been through," said guard Jackie Manuel, whose team earned the right to play fifth-seeded Georgia Tech in the semifinals today. "It meant a lot. It showed a lot."

Point guard Raymond Felton provided the points—a career-high 29—in UNC's come-from-behind victory, including all 10 points during Carolina's final 10-2, game-winning run.

But it was McCants, with 13 points in only 15 minutes, who provided the much-needed spark.

With 7:53 left and UNC trailing 71-58, the sharpshooter, who claimed he was neither nervous nor rusty despite missing so much much time, was one of five players inserted into the game in a mass substitution.

Over the next two minutes, he swished two three-point shots and dove on that loose ball during an 11-1 run that cut Clemson's lead to 72-69 with 5:50 left.

Carolina, in danger of losing the game and possibly a top seeding in the NCAA Tournament, was finally energized.

And focused.

Clemson guard Shawan Robinson said McCants's return "gave them a confidence boost, and he was a major factor in the game."

Before the game, however, McCants wasn't even sure how much he would play.

"I told him I'm not going to have a plan where he plays this many minutes at whatever time. I'm going to go by the seat of my pants," UNC coach Roy Williams said. "But I hoped I was going to be able to play him for a few stretches of two or three minutes in the first half."

McCants said sitting on the bench, in uniform for the first time in almost three weeks, was exciting but nerve-wracking, especially when UNC trailed early.

"I was like, 'When are you going to call me? When are you going to call me? When are you going to call me?'" he said. "And he called me, and I was ready."

McCants played two three-minute stretches in the first half, contributing four free throws and a layup, but missed a three-pointer. However, UNC trailed at halftime for only the fifth time this season because no one, including McCants, could slow Robinson, a Raleigh native. He had 15 points on six-for-seven shooting before the break and finished with a team-high 17.

"There were times where they made a run, and we fought back hard," Hammonds said. "They went on a run at the end, and we just did not fight back hard enough. If we had fought back harder, we could have held them off."

		1st	2nd	Total
Clemson		43	38	81
North Carolina		40	48	88

CLEMSON

Player	FGM-A	3FGM-A	FTM-A	O-D REB	A	BLK	S	TP
12 Babalola	3-7	0-3	3-4	1-2	1	0	3	9
32 Perry	2-5	0-0	2-2	0-2	0	1	0	6
5 Ford	5-8	0-0	5-8	4-4	0	1	0	15
3 Hamilton	4-9	1-2	7-8	1-3	5	0	3	16
25 Hammonds	2-9	1-6	2-5	1-2	0	0	1	7
15 Moore	2-5	0-2	1-2	1-1	2	1	2	5
22 Robinson	7-11	3-4	0-0	0-0	1	0	1	17
33 Akingbala	0-2	0-0	0-0	2-3	1	2	1	0
44 Mays	3-3	0-0	0-0	1-0	0	1	1	6

NORTH CAROLINA

Player	FGM-A	3FGM-A	FTM-A	O-D REB	A	BLK	S	TP
5 Manuel	0-2	0-1	0-0	0-1	0	0	3	0
21 J. Williams	4-7	2-4	3-3	2-2	2	0	3	13
42 May	3-10	0-0	7-9	6-0	1	1	1	13
1 Scott	2-5	1-4	2-3	0-0	1	0	3	7
2 Felton	7-15	4-6	11-16	2-5	3	0	0	29
3 Terry	0-0	0-0	0-0	0-0	0	0	0	0
11 Thomas	0-1	0-0	0-0	0-0	0	0	0	0
24 M. Williams	1-4	0-1	8-8	3-3	1	0	0	10
32 McCants	3-5	2-3	5-6	0-1	0	0	0	13
34 Noel	1-5	0-0	1-2	2-4	2	1	0	3
41 Sanders	0-0	0-0	0-0	0-0	0	0	0	0

OPPOSITE PAGE: UNC's Raymond Felton drives on Clemson's Cliff Hammonds during the first half as the Tar Heels pull off an 88-81 comeback win. Felton had a career-high 29 points
Staff Photo by Scott Lewis

If not for Felton, who scored the go-ahead three-pointer with 1:21 left. And if not for McCants, who declined to discuss details of his illness, saying only that he knew something was wrong the last time his team played Clemson.

"Before that game, I ate some bad ranch dressing...and I didn't know what it was, I couldn't really run up and down," he said.

But now, he said, he's healthy with his mom cooking meals to help him gain his weight back.

"I am 100 percent and just really glad to be back," he said.

As if you couldn't tell by that first-half floor flop. "His biggest play of the game was him diving on the floor," Williams said.

BACK TO THE DRAWING BOARD

By Robbi Pickeral

After North Carolina's 78-75 loss to Georgia Tech in the ACC semifinals, UNC center Sean May didn't want anyone to think his second-ranked team had broken down.

Just its defense, shooting, intensity, assists, and rebounding prowess.

That's why, beginning with what probably will be a grueling practice today, UNC (27-4) plans to "go back to the basics," forward Jawad Williams said, and, hopefully, master them.

A failure to do so in the NCAA Tournament would end the Tar Heels' season.

"Obviously, we can't lose from here on out," said May, adding that the Heels had played at the MCI Center as if they were "fat and happy" with their conference regular-season title.

Carolina, which hasn't won the ACC Tournament since 1998, still was expected to be one of four No. 1 seeds when the NCAA field of 65 was announced. If Georgia Tech (19-10) doesn't win the tournament title and an automatic bid, it should receive an at-large invitation, as well.

"To beat the No. 1 seed in the ACC Tournament says a lot about our guys," Yellow Jackets coach Paul Hewitt said. "This statement is not one of disrespect towards North Carolina—they are great and could very well win the national championship—but this was no upset out here today."

To win the six games necessary for a national championship, Carolina first must fix the problems that were apparent—its fewest assists of the season (nine), a beating on the boards (by seven), and a career high from the opponent's third-leading scorer (Will Bynum's 35 points).

"It was a disappointing day for us, and to be honest, I am disappointed with how we played (the past two games)," said UNC coach Roy Williams, whose top-seeded team had to overcome a 13-point deficit to beat ninth-seeded Clemson. "We're going to go back to Chapel Hill and get back out on the practice court and see if we can get better. We need to create more cohesiveness on both ends of the floor."

Of highest concern for the Tar Heels will be the defensive end, where they had shown steady improvement this season.

The fifth-seeded Yellow Jackets shot 36.9 percent, and their two leading scorers, Jarrett Jack and B.J. Elder, were a combined two-for-16.

However, Bynum, who had a concussion the last time these two teams played and missed all four of his three-point attempts, made half of his 10 shots from behind the arc this time. The Tar Heels said the lack of help and rotation on Tech's dribble penetration caused the defensive meltdown and left Bynum open too often.

So that will be a focus in practice for the Tar Heels.

Along with boxing out.

Along with sprinting to their defensive assignments earlier.

	1st	2nd	Total
Georgia Tech	42	26	78
North Carolina	36	39	75

GEORGIA TECH

Player	FGM-A	3FGM-A	FTM-A	O-D REB	A	BLK	S	TP
55 McHenry	0-1	0-0	0-0	1-1	1	2	0	0
12 Schenscher	7-13	0-0	1-1	7-3	1	3	1	15
1 Elder	0-4	0-1	2-2	0-2	0	0	0	2
3 Jack	2-12	1-3	1-4	1-8	5	0	2	6
11 Bynum	10-21	5-10	10-12	0-3	1	0	0	35
4 Dickey	1-2	0-0	3-4	1-1	1	2	0	5
5 West	1-4	0-0	2-2	4-4	0	0	0	4
23 Morrow	1-6	1-5	2-2	2-1	1	0	0	5
32 Smith	2-2	0-0	2-2	1-1	0	0	0	6
44 Tarver	0-0	0-0	0-0	0-0	0	0	0	0

NORTH CAROLINA

Player	FGM-A	3FGM-A	FTM-A	O-D REB	A	BLK	S	TP
5 Manuel	1-3	0-0	3-3	2-1	2	0	0	5
21 J. Williams	1-11	1-5	2-2	2-4	2	0	0	5
42 May	8-13	0-0	1-2	7-4	0	3	1	17
1 Scott	1-3	1-2	0-0	1-0	2	1	1	3
2 Felton	4-11	2-7	7-8	0-2	2	0	2	17
3 Terry	0-1	0-0	0-0	0-0	0	0	0	0
11 Thomas	0-0	0-0	0-0	0-0	0	0	0	0
24 M. Williams	0-3	0-1	9-10	1-4	0	0	1	9
32 McCants	6-14	4-9	1-3	0-2	1	1	0	17
34 Noel	1-2	0-0	0-0	3-1	0	0	0	2
41 Sanders	0-0	0-0	0-0	0-0	0	0	0	0

OPPOSITE PAGE: UNC's Jackie Manuel, right, fights to keep control of the ball with defensive pressure from Georgia Tech's Jarrett Jack, left, in the second half of play. Georgia Tech upset UNC 78-75. Staff Photo by Scott Lewis

Along with denying opponents the ball.

"It's the fundamental things we've been doing all year," said swingman Rashad McCants, who scored 17 points off the bench in his second game since sitting out four straight victories with an intestinal disorder.

"It's not that we need to rebuild it, it's just that we need to go out there and do it more, and do it harder, and do it more intense."

In addition to their disjointed defensive play, sixth man Marvin Williams failed to score a field goal for the first time this year; forward Jawad Williams's one-for-11 effort was his worst since he was zero-for-three his freshman season; and the Tar Heels—the highest-scoring team in the nation—shot 36.1 percent.

Still, despite all of the negative numbers, UNC had a chance to win in the final minute.

With Carolina trailing by as many as nine points in the first half and five in the second, McCants missed two free throws with 18.3 seconds left but made up for it when he buried a three from the wing to cut the deficit to 76-75 with 11 seconds left.

Bynum followed with two free throws to give the Yellow Jackets a three-point cushion with 9.6 seconds left, and on the final play of the game, McCants missed a potential tying three-pointer by about a millimeter.

"I thought it was good," McCants said, shaking his head.

But in the end, perhaps it's good that it wasn't.

UNC, May insisted, really hasn't been playing well the past couple of weeks; instead of its normal blowouts, the team had to come from behind to win its previous four games.

The loss will make them work harder, the players said—and hopefully better.

Or else.

"We have a lot to go home to watch film, break it down, regroup," said May, who led the team with 17 points and 11 rebounds. "We're going to be OK."

NCAA TOURNAMENT

LET'S GET BETTER

By Robbi Pickeral

After top-seeded North Carolina shot 73.3 percent, dished out 19 assists, and led No. 16 Oakland (Michigan) by 26 points in the first half, UNC coach Roy Williams gave his team this instruction:

"Let's get better."

So, after the Tar Heels gave the ball away on three of their first five possessions in the second half, it wasn't surprising to see all five starters on the bench.

"It's not OK to just turn it over and say, 'Oh, well, we've got a 25-point lead,'" said Williams, who also had pulled his starters en masse during UNC's previous two games. "We're not going to have that [every game]."

By blowing out the Golden Grizzlies 96-68 at Charlotte Coliseum—with the starting five eventually back out on the court—UNC earned the right to face ninth-seeded Iowa State in the second round of the NCAA Tournament.

Unlike Oakland, the Tar Heels (28-4) may not be able to afford mental lapses, silly turnovers, or defensive letdowns in the coming rounds of the tournament, even for two or three minutes.

"He wants perfection...so do we," said shooting guard Melvin Scott, who returned to the reserve corps after Rashad McCants started for the first time in seven games.

They proved they had their energy back when, leading 13-5, freshman Marvin Williams swatted an Oakland pass, prevented the ball from going out of bounds on the sideline and then watched as sprinting teammate Raymond Felton kept the ball from going out on the baseline by flicking it backward to trailing Jackie Manuel.

Manuel grabbed it, laid it in, and was fouled.

"A couple of turnovers we made early got the game going too fast," Golden Grizzlies coach Greg Kampe said. "Boy, they played good."

UNC proved it had its teamwork back, recording 14 assists on its first 14 baskets and finishing with 27. In two games last weekend, Carolina had only 19.

	1st	2nd	Total
Oakland	33	35	68
North Carolina	59	37	96

OAKLAND

Player	FGM-A	3FGM-A	FTM-A	O-D REB	A	BLK	S	TP
1 Marshall	5-17	0-3	6-10	3-2	0	0	2	16
44 McCloskey	3-3	0-0	1-2	2-1	0	0	1	7
52 Scott	8-16	0-0	5-6	3-3	4	0	2	21
3 Dukes	0-0	0-0	0-0	1-2	0	0	0	0
10 Ishmael	2-6	2-3	0-0	0-0	7	0	1	6
2 Coleman	0-0	0-0	0-0	0-0	0	0	0	0
12 Cassise	5-10	4-8	0-0	0-1	0	0	3	14
24 Carson	2-5	0-1	0-0	0-0	1	0	0	4
40 Ritzema	0-1	0-0	0-0	0-1	0	0	0	0

NORTH CAROLINA

Player	FGM-A	3FGM-A	FTM-A	O-D REB	A	BLK	S	TP
21 J. Williams	4-6	1-1	0-0	2-0	1	1	0	9
32 McCants	6-9	4-6	0-0	2-0	2	0	1	16
42 May	6-12	0-0	7-9	5-3	1	0	0	19
2 Felton	2-5	2-5	0-0	0-4	7	0	1	6
5 Manuel	5-6	0-0	0-3	3-0	4	0	1	10
0 Holley	0-1	0-0	0-0	1-2	1	0	0	0
1 Scott	2-2	2-2	0-0	1-1	3	0	1	6
3 Terry	2-2	1-1	0-1	0-0	0	0	2	5
11 Thomas	0-0	0-0	0-0	0-2	4	0	0	0
15 Everett	0-0	0-0	0-0	0-0	0	0	0	0
22 Miller	1-2	1-2	0-0	0-0	1	0	0	3
24 M. Williams	8-11	1-2	3-4	0-8	1	2	2	20
34 Noel	0-0	0-0	0-0	0-2	2	0	1	0
35 Hooker	0-0	0-0	0-2	0-0	0	0	0	0
41 Sanders	1-2	0-0	0-0	0-0	0	0	0	2

ABOVE: UNC's Marvin Williams goes for a rebound against Oakland's Patrick McCloskey during the Syracuse Regional's opening round. Staff Photo by Scott Lewis

"We just wanted to go out there and share the ball and prove we are a good team," said McCants, who made six of his nine shots and scored 16 points.

"It's all about taking care of business," said Manuel, who had 10 points and three rebounds.

Starting power forward Jawad Williams played 19 minutes and stretched his hip flexor every time he left the game. He had nine points and two rebounds.

"Raymond playing 24 minutes may be the fewest minutes he's played in a long time," Roy Williams said. "So we did want to keep the minutes down, but I was sort of fighting a little battle, because I wanted us to keep playing, to keep sharp, but the score was a little bit out of hand and I wanted to keep the guys fresh…Who knows? Sometimes it works out, sometimes it doesn't."

"I thought Illinois, [the No. 1 seed in the Chicago Regional], was the best team in the country when we played them," Kampe said. "But tonight was a clinic, as good as it gets."

WEARING OUT THE CYCLONES

By Robbi Pickeral

Being a freshman, North Carolina forward Marvin Williams never experienced an 8-20 season like his senior teammates, a coaching switch like the juniors or even an NCAA second-round disappointment like the sophomores.

However, earning a berth in the NCAA round of 16 with a 92-65 victory over Iowa State meant just as much to him, Williams said, "Because I could be part of something that was so important to them."

And he showed it.

Top-seeded UNC is advancing to the second weekend of the NCAA Tournament for the first time since 2000 partly because the ACC Freshman of the Year shot over and dunked through the Cyclones' active press, contributed a double-double by halftime and simply wore the under-manned ninth-seeded opponent down.

Then out.

The Tar Heels (29-4) will play No. 5 seed Villanova at the Carrier Dome in Syracuse, New York, for the right to play in the regional final.

"The kid just plays with a lot of passion and fire," said center Sean May, adding that Williams's play helped open things up for him to get a team-high 24 points and 17 rebounds. "...He can't help the talent he has; he just gets it done."

Williams had 20 points and 15 rebounds after contributing 20 points and eight rebounds against Oakland in the first round.

And what continues to drown opponents such as Iowa State (19-12) is this: He does it off the bench.

"When we sub, there's a lot of ways our team gets better," said UNC coach Roy Williams, who has now led teams to the round of 16 ten times. "We were a little more fresh, and that helps with the way we like to play."

UNC got better with Williams on the floor because of his versatility. His first two field goals were three-pointers, which helped the Tar Heels pull ahead 15-13. But his agile athleticism also helped him snake his way through Iowa State's trapping zone to score on putbacks and short jumpers, alike.

Iowa State chipped its deficit 36-33 with 3:02 left in the first half when freshman Rahshon Clark scored in transition. But the Cyclones failed to score on their

OPPOSITE PAGE: UNC's Sean May leaps past Iowa State's Curtis Stinson, left, and Jared Homan for one of his 17 rebounds as the Tar Heels win easily, 92-65. May was the game's high scorer with 24 points. Staff Photo by Scott Lewis

final seven possessions of the half, missing the front end of two one-and-ones and watching a three-pointer rim out.

Meanwhile, the seemingly tireless Marvin Williams had two field goals during the Tar Heels' half-ending 9-0 run that culminated in a three-pointer from Raymond Felton (15 points, eight assists) that was released at least five feet behind the three-point arc.

The Tar Heels took a 45-33 lead into halftime, then opened the second half with a 10-2 run that included a jump shot, a block, and a steal by Marvin Williams.

"In the locker room, Jackie [Manuel] just told us, 'Most of the year, we've come out flat after halftime.'" May said. "He just said, 'We're not coming out flat after halftime.'"

The Tar Heels didn't. And Iowa State, which pulled its three-quarter-court trapping zone back to a halfcourt set early in the game, never threatened again.

"They're just deep—that's what makes them really good," said Cyclones guard Curtis Stinson. "...Of course, it's going to help them when they keep rotating these guys like that."

Marvin Williams's flourish was also important because starting power forward Jawad Williams struggled. The senior was 0-for-6, but he didn't blame his injured hip.

Carolina also only made 14 of 25 shots from the free-throw line, something else it will work on in preparation for Villanova.

Marvin Williams, however, has little to work on after his first NCAA weekend. Except, maybe, resting up for the next one.

"I've been blessed," he said. "We've all been blessed to get to the second week of the tournament, and hopefully, we can get even farther."

For his teammates. And for himself.

OPPOSITE PAGE: UNC's Jawad Williams gets double-teamed by Iowa State's Tasheed Carr (10) and Curtis Stinson in the second half. The Tar Heels advanced with a 92-65 drubbing of the Cyclones. *Staff Photo by Chuck Liddy*

	1st	2nd	Total
Iowa State	33	32	65
North Carolina	45	47	92

IOWA STATE

Player	FGM-A	3FGM-A	FTM-A	O-D REB	A	BLK	S	TP
13 Clark	6-9	1-3	0-2	2-2	1	0	1	13
22 Staple	3-7	0-1	0-3	3-2	1	0	0	6
51 Homan	8-19	0-0	3-5	5-15	1	2	1	19
1 Stinson	6-17	1-2	1-3	5-2	7	0	4	14
11 Blalock	2-12	1-3	0-0	1-5	6	0	1	5
3 Neal	0-0	0-0	0-0	0-0	0	0	0	0
10 Carr	2-11	1-4	3-4	1-0	4	0	0	8
30 Agnew	0-0	0-0	0-0	0-0	0	0	0	0
31 Streff	0-0	0-0	0-0	0-0	0	0	0	0
34 Bergstrom	0-1	0-0	0-0	0-0	0	0	1	0
40 Braet	0-0	0-0	0-0	0-0	0	0	0	0

NORTH CAROLINA

Player	FGM-A	3FGM-A	FTM-A	O-D REB	A	BLK	S	TP
21 J. Williams	0-6	0-2	1-5	2-2	1	0	2	1
32 McCants	6-13	2-5	3-6	0-2	4	0	1	17
42 May	8-9	0-0	8-9	7-10	2	1	3	24
2 Felton	5-12	3-6	2-4	1-3	8	1	3	15
5 Manuel	1-4	0-1	4-6	1-1	0	0	1	6
0 Holley	1-1	0-0	0-0	0-0	0	0	1	2
1 Scott	2-6	1-5	0-0	0-0	3	0	0	5
3 Terry	0-0	0-0	0-0	0-1	0	0	0	0
11 Thomas	0-0	0-0	0-0	0-0	1	0	0	0
15 Everett	0-0	0-0	1-1	0-0	0	0	0	1
22 Miller	0-1	0-1	1-1	0-1	0	0	0	1
24 M. Williams	8-12	2-4	2-3	2-13	0	1	2	20
34 Noel	0-1	0-1	0-2	0-0	1	0	1	0
35 Hooker	0-0	0-0	0-0	0-1	0	0	0	0
41 Sanders	0-0	0-0	0-0	0-0	0	1	0	0

A CLOSE CALL

By Robbi Pickeral

Even on the bench, frustrated and fouled out, North Carolina point guard Raymond Felton was trying to be his team's leader when they needed it the most.

"I almost lost it out there," senior Jawad Williams said after his top-seeded team pulled out a 67-66 victory over No. 5 Villanova at the Carrier Dome. "But [Raymond] told me we were going to pull it out."

Somehow they did—by the skin of their point-guard-less teeth. The Tar Heels overcame a first-half, 12-point deficit—and the loss of their floor leader in the second half—to advance to the NCAA round of eight for the first time since 1999-2000.

"In situations like that, we got to learn to win ugly, and that's what we did," said senior Melvin Scott, who played Felton's minutes down the stretch.

Carolina, which had several starters in foul trouble by the end of the first half, had battled back to take its biggest lead of the game, 50-45, when Felton picked up his fourth foul on a reach-in with 8:26 left. He immediately went to the bench, and freshman Quentin Thomas, who hadn't played in the first half, checked in.

That didn't last long. After Thomas immediately committed an offensive foul, he was replaced by senior Melvin Scott. Villanova's Randy Foye then scored on a drive.

On the Wildcats' next possession, Scott got beat on the dribble by Kyle Lowry and fouled him for a three-point play attempt. Lowry's free throw knotted the score at 50.

But somehow, with their floor leader still on the bench, UNC managed to reel off an 11-0 run, thanks to nine points from swingman Rashad McCants.

"I told him I was going to give him the ball and he had to carry us," Scott said. "...We just wanted him to get aggressive offensively and attack...and I got him the rock. That's my job."

Leading 59-50, the Tar Heels looked as if they had dodged a bullet...until Felton re-entered the game, picked up his fifth and final foul with 2:11 left, and headed to the bench for good. It was the first time in his college career he had fouled out.

OPPOSITE PAGE: UNC's Rashad McCants is sandwiched by Villanova's Will Sheridan, left, Randy Foye, center, and Mike Nardi in the first half. Staff Photo by Scott Lewis

"I thought there was more of a panic when Raymond went out the second time," UNC coach Roy Williams said. "I thought there was a sense of calmness the first time, but they were not as calm as I wanted them to be the second time."

Villanova point guard Mike Nardi immediately buried a three-pointer, cutting the lead to 64-59. Two more free throws by the Wildcats cut it to 64-61. And yet another cut it to 64-62 with 40 seconds left.

Scott, playing point guard again, was fouled with 28.9 seconds, and made two free throws to give UNC a four-point cushion.

But the final, frenetic 18 seconds included an offensive rebound by Villanova off a free throw, and a running field goal by Wildcat Allan Ray that was waved off because of a traveling violation.

That had the crowd calling foul.

"I drove to the basket, and I thought the ref had called a foul, but he called traveling," Ray said. "We should never have been in that position. I can't say the reason we lost is because of that play."

In the end, McCants led the Tar Heels with 17 points. Center Sean May (14 points, 10 rebounds) and Felton (11 points, 11 rebounds) both finished with double-doubles.

Carolina opened the second half with its ninth turnover of the game, then allowed six-foot freshman Lowry to slide in for consecutive offensive rebounds.

Coach Williams wasn't pleased. At the 15:08 mark, after Will Sheridan dunked for Villanova to make it 40-37, Williams tore off his jacket, thought about tossing it into the crowd, then angrily yanked off his glasses, instead, before joining the timeout huddle.

Despite UNC's continued sub-par play, Felton tied it for only the third time of the game, this time 42-42, when he buried a three-pointer with 12:23 left. With May back on the bench with three fouls, freshman forward Marvin Williams gave Carolina its first lead, 44-42, with 11:43 left, when he buried two free throws.

The Tar Heels had been worried that the Wildcats would increase their intensity and better their play without junior forward Curtis Sumpter, the team's leading scorer who tore the anterior cruciate ligament in his left knee last weekend. With Sumpter out, the Wildcats started Lowry, and their four-guard lineup worked early.

Carolina dug as much as a 21-9 hole within the first nine minutes of the game, and by halftime, just about everything that could go wrong for the Tar Heels, had.

Four of UNC's top players had two fouls apiece, including their top two rebounders, Marvin Williams and May, who spent much of the latter part of the half on the bench.

Villanova got 17 points from sharpshooter Foye—and with Marvin Williams and May on the bench, UNC had to sit back in a zone on several possessions (and the Wildcats still shot over it).

OPPOSITE PAGE: UNC's Sean May gets fouled by Villanova's Will Sheridan in the first half of their Sweet Sixteen match-up. Staff Photo by Scott Lewis

Meanwhile, the Tar Heels' sharpest shooters were their dullest, as McCants was 1-for-6, and Felton was 1-for-8.

The only thing that started going right was in the final 6:23 of the first half, when the Tar Heels outscored the Wildcats 10-3 by holding Villanova without a field goal (the Wildcats were 0-for-8 during that span).

OPPOSITE PAGE: UNC's Melvin Scott celebrates after traveling was called on Villanova's Allan Ray with seconds left in their game during UNC's 67-66 victory in their Sweet Sixteen game at the Carrier Dome at Syracuse University.
Staff Photo by Ethan Hyman

BELOW: From the bench, UNC's Raymond Felton eyes the scoreboard during the last tense few seconds of the Tar Heels' 67-66 win over Villanova despite his fouling out.
Staff Photo by Scott Lewis

	1st	2nd	Total
Villanova	33	33	66
North Carolina	29	38	67

VILLANOVA

Player	FGM-A	3FGM-A	FTM-A	O-D REB	A	BLK	S	TP
2 Foye	9-21	5-12	5-7	2-1	2	0	2	28
50 Sheridan	2-3	0-0	0-0	1-4	0	2	0	4
12 Nardi	2-8	1-4	1-2	0-1	1	0	0	6
13 Lowry	7-10	1-2	3-5	3-4	3	1	2	18
14 Ray	2-14	1-10	2-2	0-3	1	0	0	7
20 Fraser	1-4	0-0	1-3	3-3	0	2	1	3
44 Austin	0-1	0-0	0-0	3-1	0	0	0	0

NORTH CAROLINA

Player	FGM-A	3FGM-A	FTM-A	O-D REB	A	BLK	S	TP
21 J. Williams	1-4	0-2	0-0	1-1	1	0	0	2
32 McCants	3-9	2-5	9-10	2-1	1	0	0	17
42 May	6-9	0-0	2-3	2-8	1	0	1	14
2 Felton	4-12	3-7	0-2	3-8	5	0	0	11
5 Manuel	1-4	0-1	0-0	0-3	0	2	0	2
1 Scott	1-1	1-1	2-2	0-2	2	0	0	5
24 M. Williams	4-9	2-3	6-6	2-3	0	0	1	16
34 Noel	0-0	0-0	0-1	0-2	1	1	1	0

CARRIER DOME IN SYRACUSE, NY

MARCHING ON

By Robbi Pickeral

Laughing, hugging and flashing four fingers— "Regional Champions" T-shirt wrapped around his neck and matching hat sitting askew on his head—North Carolina center Sean May didn't mind waiting his turn to cut down the nets at the Carrier Dome.

After all, he had spent plenty of time around the rim all day.

"You have to experience this to really know what it feels like to go to the Final Four," an exuberant May said after scoring 29 points and grabbing 12 rebounds to lead top-seeded UNC to an 88-82 victory over No. six seed Wisconsin.

"This is what it's about. This is why you get up in the morning and run sprints. This is why you go through gut checks in the middle of the season. It's an incredible feeling."

Carolina will play Michigan State in the national semifinals in St. Louis because it survived early foul problems and a late ankle tweak to point guard Raymond Felton; it got timely clutch plays from swingman Rashad McCants; and the Tar Heels made seven of eight free throws in the final minute to seal it.

But the no. 1 key was the lane domination of May, who was named the Syracuse Regional's MVP.

"I told him I was his biggest cheerleader out there," said Melvin Scott, one of three seniors who persevered through an 8-20 record their freshman season with the hope that this experience would come. "I probably needed some pompoms because I kept saying 'Get the ball to Sean! Get the ball to Sean!' because they couldn't stop him.

"And after the game, he said, 'That was for you, man.'"

The gregarious May, rarely fretful during any game, acknowledged that he was nervous the night before this one. He didn't get to bed until about 2:15 in the morning, he said, because "I just kept running the game through my mind, situations that were probably going to happen."

Any lingering jitters didn't show.

The burly junior dominated from the outset, scoring on four of North Carolina's first five possessions

and getting 16 points and six rebounds en route to a 44-33 lead with 2:59 left in the first half.

At first, he made the game look as if it would be a Tar Heels runaway.

But with Felton on the bench with two fouls—and the Badgers packing their defense into the lane because they didn't have to worry about Felton—UNC had trouble passing the ball to May, and the only scoring attempt he made the rest of the half was a missed jump shot.

Meanwhile, Wisconsin scored the final 11 points of the opening half take a 44-44 deadlock into half-time.

It was a runaway no more.

"Coach [Joe] Holladay just told me at halftime, 'We're going to have to ride your back a little bit,'" May said.

No worries. He is six feet nine inches and weighs 260 pounds.

Wisconsin opened the second half with five straight points, extending its run to 16-0 and grabbing its biggest lead of the game. But with 17:30 left, Felton fed May for a three-point play, beginning a 14-0 Tar Heels counter-run that included two more lay-ups from the big man to give North Carolina a 58-49 advantage.

"There aren't too many guys built like him, and he knows how to use what he has," Badgers coach Bo Ryan said. "...May has scored on a lot of teams, and he works at it. And a lot of us as coaches, we tell our guys to get to ball to those kind of guys. We do it. They did it."

Still, the undersized Badgers never folded.

Wisconsin cut the deficit to one point on two occasions during the final seven minutes, and had a chance to tie it with 2:23 left, when guard Clayton Hanson cocked his hand for a three-pointer, only to have it blocked cleanly by McCants.

May (who else?) followed that with two free throws, and Carolina led by at least three points the rest of the way, despite 25 points from Wisconsin forward Alando Tucker.

"We're ecstatic," said UNC coach Roy Williams, who has made four previous trips to the Final Four but has yet to win a national title. "It is one of the greatest feelings as a coach, the look on your guys' faces when they accomplish something, especially when it was difficult. And needless to say, against Villanova and against Wisconsin, it was very difficult."

UNC's victory marks the sixth time the Tar Heels have reached the Final Four as a No. 1 seed—including 1982 and 1993, when they won national titles. It also marks UNC's seventh consecutive victory in NCAA regional final games.

The trip to St. Louis will mark the first Final Four for all of the players, including May—who answered questions after the game with a net around his neck, and a cutting from it tucked under his cap.

May now has posted 11 double-doubles in Carolina's past 13 games, but he said the net will go

OPPOSITE PAGE: UNC's Jackie Manuel is tied up with Wisconsin's Alando Tucker during Tar Heels' 88-82 win over the Badgers to capture the Syracuse Regional Championship and advance to the NCAA Final Four in St. Louis.
Staff Photo by Scott Lewis

to one of the seniors, who have inspired him all year—and who were the first to get the scissors as the clock wound down and the celebration began.

"Every day, I look at Melvin, Jawad [Williams], and Jackie [Manuel] and try to do my part to help prolong their careers," May said. "To set these goals and to reach these goals, especially at this level, it says a lot about the character of this program, and myself, and the players that are here."

OPPOSITE PAGE: UNC's Sean May celebrates with Marvin Williams afterUNC's 88-82 victory over Wisconsin. Staff Photo by Ethan Hyman

BELOW: UNC's Sean May slams home two of his game-high 29 points in the first half as UNC defeated Wisconsin 88-82 in the Syracuse Regional Finals to advance to the Final Four. May was named Tournament MVP. Staff Photo by Ethan Hyman

	1st	2nd	Total
Wisconsin	44	38	82
North Carolina	44	44	88

WISCONSIN

Player	FGM-A	3FGM-A	FTM-A	O-D REB	A	BLK	S	TP
42 Tucker	9-17	0-4	7-9	1-1	2	0	1	25
44 Morley	0-1	0-0	0-0	0-3	3	0	1	0
54 Wilkinson	5-11	1-2	0-0	3-4	5	0	2	11
1 Chambliss	3-7	3-6	0-0	0-3	4	0	0	9
13 Hanson	5-8	5-8	0-0	2-0	1	0	0	15
4 Nixon	1-2	0-0	0-0	1-0	0	0	0	2
21 Helmigk	0-1	0-0	0-0	0-1	1	0	0	0
22 Flowers	0-1	0-1	0-0	1-1	0	0	0	0
23 Taylor	6-12	2-3	4-4	0-3	1	0	0	18
32 Butch	0-0	0-0	0-0	0-1	0	0	0	0
34 Stiemsma	1-1	0-0	0-0	0-0	0	0	0	2

NORTH CAROLINA

Player	FGM-A	3FGM-A	FTM-A	O-D REB	A	BLK	S	TP
21 J. Williams	3-6	0-3	0-0	0-2	1	1	0	6
32 McCants	8-17	3-6	2-4	2-2	4	1	0	21
42 May	13-19	0-0	3-4	5-7	2	2	0	29
2 Felton	5-11	1-5	6-6	1-4	7	1	0	17
5 Manuel	2-2	0-0	0-0	2-0	1	0	3	4
1 Scott	1-1	1-1	0-0	0-0	1	0	0	3
11 Thomas	0-0	0-0	0-0	0-0	1	0	0	0
24 M. Williams	1-6	0-1	4-4	0-3	1	0	2	6
34 Noel	1-2	0-0	0-0	1-2	1	0	0	2

ROY WILLIAMS

By Caulton Tudor

The pressure to win big never will be off Roy Williams. That sort of thing goes with having the keys to the North Carolina basketball coach's office.

But for now, Williams should be allowed to relax and enjoy the ride that he's earned. Getting there, in this case, was the ultimate journey for the Carolina program that Williams was handed.

Granted, he was handed a lot of talent, but team routinely trumps talent in college basketball, and particularly in the rat maze that is the NCAA Tournament.

The Tar Heels that Williams greeted at the outset of the 2003-04 season were not much of a team.

About 16 months later, after a semifinal loss in the ACC Tournament, there was room to doubt whether William's second UNC team was good enough to make an extended run in the NCAA Tournament.

But in the Carrier Dome, Williams and his players finally saw the end of the long road back.

Against a Wisconsin opponent that personified the definition of team and teamwork, the Tar Heels pulled out the kind of effort and unity that for decades had made the program famous.

The 88-82 victory was largely made possible by a blocked shot by Rashad McCants, second-effort rebounding by Sean May and Jackie Manuel, and clutch free-throw shooting by Raymond Felton.

The bigger the stakes, the more important the little things. Carolina showed a rich appreciation for that fact in the Syracuse Regional championship.

But at ground level, this could have been Carolina's first Final Four visit. So thoroughly had the link to the coaching eras of Frank McGuire, Dean Smith, and Bill Guthridge been severed that Williams might as well have been taking over UCLA. Or Enron.

"He's taught, and we've listened," May said.

Williams has said on any number of occasions that had May not been injured early in his freshman year ('02-'03), Matt Doherty would still be the coach at Carolina, and Williams would still be at Kansas.

There's some truth in those words. Doherty's last team, even without May most of the season, began to show signs of a recovery and finished a competitive 19-16.

But equally true is the fact that under Doherty, the devotion to detail and pride slipped. Much of it wasn't his fault as coach. He had what amounted to a freshman and sophomore team that was grasping for direction. Doherty just didn't have the experience and coaching background to set that direction properly.

Williams did, but he still had to instill direction in a group of players that he did not recruit, nor know very well.

And by no means has it been a bump-free run. As late as the final 90 seconds of the first half, he was slapping hands emotionally in McCants's face after the player had retreated into loose defense and careless shot selection.

With 2:23 left in the game, McCants made what for years at UNC may be remembered as "the stuff." He swatted away an attempt by Wisconsin's Clayton Hanson, recovered the ball in the mid-air and fed May for a possession that led to a 78-73 lead.

Those two moments—Williams's reprimand in the first half and McCants's block—defined how far Carolina had made it back.

"These kids went through a lot...through something that no one at North Carolina has ever done," Williams said. "I saw that from a distance. It's special for me, my assistants, and our families. But it's really special for those...kids, and I'll just leave it at that."

Great coaches have to be defined in the long run by great achievements. At the college level, that normally means a national championship ring, and it's not likely to change dramatically.

Williams doesn't have a ring. He may never get one. For years, there was a feeling that Dean Smith and Mike Krzyzewski wouldn't. Gene Keady ended his coaching career without having reached a Final Four.

But coaches can achieve great things without claiming the ultimate prize. In his second season, Ol' Roy restored a part of Carolina's basketball birthright.

Even for the most demanding of Tar Heels fans, that should be plenty good enough.

Staff Photo by Scott Lewis

Name: Roy Williams
Born: August 1, 1950
Hometown: Biltmore, North Carolina
Attended: University of North
Carolina, Graduated 1972

FINAL FOUR

EDWARDS JONES DOME IN ST. LOUIS, MO

HEELS ONE WIN AWAY

By Robbi Pickeral

As the clock wound down on North Carolina's 87-71 victory against Michigan State at the Edward Jones Dome, Sean May congratulated teammate Jawad Williams with something better than an embrace.

"Jawad," junior told the senior, smile on his face, "The reason why we won this game is because you have heart, and you wouldn't let us fail."

UNC (32-4) will face Illinois in the NCAA national championship game because the forward who never made excuses for his recent poor play would hear no excuse for why he couldn't extend his college career one more game.

On a night when center May struggled early and freshman sixth man Marvin Williams barely showed up in the box score, it was Jawad Williams—whose injury-plagued final third of the season had some questioning why he was even still starting—who was the constant.

His 20 points were his most since late February. His eight rebounds was his best since mid-January.

Guess that injured left hip flexor is feeling better, after all.

"He was a totally different player than what I've seen the last four games," May said. "He's that old Jawad Williams—dunking on people, rebounding the ball, making big plays, and doing the little things that it takes to win that he probably doesn't get enough credit for."

Williams, who had scored in double figures only once his previous eight games, had 12 points and six rebounds by halftime, when UNC trailed 38-33. Without him, the Tar Heels might have trailed by more, considering they didn't pound the ball inside, took too many three-pointers and simply weren't aggressive enough, according to coach Roy Williams.

"It was un-North Carolina in the first half," said Coach Williams, who will coach in his third NCAA national final—and for his first title. "I did point that out to them at halftime."

Loudly.

And the point stuck.

Jawad Williams's alley-oop dunk barely two minutes into the second half gave the Tar Heels the lead back, 39-38. His jump shot three possessions later gave UNC a 46-42 advantage. And his field goal with 14:55 left, which gave UNC a 51-49 lead, began a 18-

OPPOSITE PAGE: UNC's Jawad Williams blocks a shot by Michigan State's Alan Anderson during UNC's 87-71 win in the semi-finals of the Final Four tournament at the Edward Jones Dome. *Staff Photo by Scott Lewis*

5 Tar Heels run that also included eight points from May and a block from—who else?

Jawad Williams.

That run gave the energized Heels a 67-52 lead with 10:18 left.

And with Jawad Williams and Marvin Williams (two points, eight rebounds) clamping down on the Spartans' Alan Anderson—MSU's second leading scorer who finished 0-for-4 with zero points— Michigan State never cut it to single digits.

"In North Carolina, I was really impressed," said Michigan State coach Tom Izzo, whose team advanced to its fourth Final Four in seven years. "If Jawad Williams plays like that—you know I think he's had [nine] points in four games, and he had 20 tonight—that's another whole dimension for them."

The 2005 national championship game will mark only the sixth time teams ranked No. 1 (the Illini) and No. 2 (the Tar Heels) at the end of the season in The Associated Press poll will play in the title game. The others occurred in 1949 (Kentucky-Oklahoma State), 1957 (UNC-Kansas), 1961 (Ohio State-Cincinnati), 1965 (Michigan-UCLA), and 1975 (UCLA-Kentucky).

It will also mark the end of a full circle for Jawad Williams, who was a freshman member of the 2001-02 team that finished 8-20.

To win a national championship, he said recently, would be "just incredible." Which is why, as the clock wound down against the Spartans, it was not surprising that he didn't show much emotion.

"Confident, like always," he said, explaining the way he felt. "But not cocky."

And quietly thrilled to have one game left.

In the end, Jawad Williams didn't lead in scoring—May did that with 22 points, while Rashad McCants chipped in 17, and Felton added 16. But he tied

"The reason why we won this game is because you have heart, and you wouldn't let us fail."

—Sean May

OPPOSITE PAGE: UNC's Sean May bolts past Michigan State's Shannon Brown during the Tar Heels' 87-71 win in the semi-finals of the Final Four tournament at the Edward Jones Dome.
Staff Photo by Scott Lewis

"I never made excuses, and I never will."

—Jawad Williams

Felton and Marvin Williams with a team-high eight rebounds.

And in the end, according to his teammates, he led the Tar Heels where they needed it most: The heart.

"The only thing I really went through [the last few weeks] is people trying to make excuses for me," said Jawad Williams, who has played through two twisted knees and a hip flexor injury. "I never made excuses, and I never will. Tonight was a great win for us, and that's all I really care about."

	1st	2nd	Total
Michigan State	38	33	71
North Carolina	33	54	87

MICHIGAN STATE

Player	FGM-A	3FGM-A	FTM-A	O-D REB	A	BLK	S	TP
15 Anderson	0-4	0-0	0-0	1-3	0	0	1	0
40 Davis	6-16	0-1	2-4	5-10	1	1	3	14
3 Brown	6-14	3-6	0-0	0-1	1	0	1	15
12 Neitzel	1-3	0-1	0-1	0-3	3	0	0	2
13 Ager	6-18	2-6	10-10	1-2	1	1	0	24
5 Hill	1-6	1-5	0-0	0-1	2	0	2	3
20 Trannon	1-1	0-0	2-2	1-2	0	1	1	4
22 Hamo	0-0	0-0	0-0	1-0	0	0	0	0
23 Torbert	4-11	1-4	0-0	2-3	6	1	2	9
30 Bograkos	0-0	0-0	0-1	1-0	0	0	0	0
34 Naymick	0-1	0-0	0-0	2-2	1	0	0	0
43 Harvey	0-0	0-0	0-0	0-0	0	0	0	0
50 Rowley	0-0	0-0	0-0	0-0	0	0	0	0

NORTH CAROLINA

Player	FGM-A	3FGM-A	FTM-A	O-D REB	A	BLK	S	TP
21 J. Williams	9-13	2-5	0-0	1-7	0	1	0	20
32 McCants	7-11	2-3	1-2	2-4	4	1	1	17
42 May	9-18	0-0	4-6	2-5	3	1	1	22
2 Felton	6-12	2-6	2-2	1-7	7	0	1	16
5 Manuel	0-1	0-0	0-0	2-1	0	0	1	0
0 Holley	0-1	0-1	0-0	0-1	0	0	0	0
1 Scott	0-2	0-2	4-4	0-2	0	0	0	4
3 Terry	1-2	0-1	0-0	0-0	0	0	0	2
11 Thomas	0-0	0-0	0-0	1-0	1	0	0	0
15 Everett	0-0	0-0	0-0	0-0	0	0	0	0
22 Miller	0-0	0-0	0-0	0-0	0	0	0	0
24 M. Williams	1-6	0-1	0-0	1-7	1	1	0	2
34 Noel	2-5	0-1	0-3	3-1	2	2	1	4
35 Hooker	0-0	0-0	0-0	0-0	0	0	0	0

OPPOSITE PAGE: UNC's Jawad Williams dunks over Michigan State's Drew Naymick, left, and Alan Anderson during UNC's 87-71 win in the semi-finals of the Final Four tournament at the Edward Jones Dome. Williams came out of a month-long slump in the game and had 20 points, eight rebounds, and a block. *Staff Photo by Scott Lewis*

NCAA CHAMPIONSHIP GAME

EDWARDS JONES DOME IN ST. LOUIS, MO

UNC IS BACK!

Tar Heels Are National Champions
Three Years After 8-20 Finish

By Robbi Pickeral

From the beginning of the season, North Carolina had a goal, and a motto: "It's amazing what can be accomplished if no one cares who gets the credit."

That's why center Sean May, despite his game-high 26 points and 10 rebounds and his tournament MVP trophy, wouldn't take credit for North Carolina's fourth national championship.

Nor would freshman Marvin Williams, who scored UNC's go-ahead basket on a tip-in with less than two minutes left.

Nor would point guard Raymond Felton, who came up with a key steal and three straight free throws to seal UNC's 75-70 victory over Illinois in the final 50 seconds of the NCAA title game.

"We came out tonight and we proved that we are a team," said Felton, who finished with 17 points, seven assists, and three rebounds at the Edward Jones Dome. "We are talented...but we are together, too, as one. That's why we have a national championship."

In a contest widely billed as talent vs. teamwork—a comparison that irritated Tar Heels, considering they had worked so hard this season to become a team—UNC proved it had both.

Junior sharpshooter Rashad McCants scored 14 points in the first half to help the Tar Heels build a 13-point lead—and didn't mind that he failed to score a single point in the second.

Senior Jackie Manuel continued to play the hard-nosed defense that made him beloved to coach Roy Williams from the get-go—the same defense that distracted Illinois guard Luther Head enough to miss a potential game-tying three-point shot with 16 seconds left.

Senior Melvin Scott came off the bench to play point guard when Felton was in foul trouble. Senior starter Jawad Williams finished the game beside Scott—and, as usual, didn't mind sharing the minutes with the freshman Williams yet again.

And there was UNC coach Roy Williams, celebrating his first NCAA title after four previous trips to the Final Four because, in his second year as UNC's head coach, he had finally instilled the team concept.

Not that he would take credit, either.

OPPOSITE PAGE: UNC's Raymond Felton races up-court against Illinois' Dee Brown during the second half during the 2005 NCAA National Basketball Championship. *Staff Photo by Scott Lewis*

"I didn't know if we had a great chance," said Williams, whose team was ranked second in the country. "I just love this team as a family. Our guys stood up and made the big shots. We went out there and won it as a team."

Top-ranked Illinois (37-2), which shot a season-worst 27 percent in the first half, led only twice—2-0 and 17-16—but battled back despite the inside dominance of May by shooting 51.5 percent after halftime.

However, after Marvin Williams tipped back a missed shot by McCants to give Carolina a 72-70 lead with 1:27 left, the Illini had several chances to tie the score. Head and Deron Williams, who had 17 points, both missed three-point shots on two separate possessions before Felton stepped in front of a pass from Head that was intended for Deron Williams.

Felton sped up the court, was fouled, buried a free throw and gave UNC a 73-70 advantage with 25.8 seconds left.

"That," said May, "was the play of the game."

Felton said, "It just boils down to what Coach has been saying all season: 'Do whatever it takes to win. Make it happen.' That's what I did."

With 16 seconds left and the Tar Heels' reserves on their feet, Head, who wound up with 21 points, missed one more three-pointer. With nine seconds left and the Illini reserves burying their heads in their hands, Felton made two more free throws before pumping his arm and looking to the stands at his family.

As the clock wound down, there was celebration, and there were tears.

"I'll remember the year, the journey," said Illinois coach Bruce Weber. "It's been unbelievable."

UNC also won national titles in 1957 under coach Frank McGuire and in 1982 and 1993 under Roy Williams' mentor, Dean Smith.

The victory also marks the end of a full circle for Carolina's three scholarship seniors—Jawad Williams, Manuel, and Scott—who persevered through an 8-20 season in 2001-02 and helped bring UNC back to the top of the college basketball world.

The question now for North Carolina (33-4) is just how much of its team will return next season. Williams, Manuel, and Scott will all graduate this summer.

Felton, a junior, said that he would "consider" going to the NBA.

McCants said, "I've got a title now; I'm going to explore my options."

Marvin Williams said he would discuss his options with coach Roy Williams after the season. And May said he would consider going only if he were a top-10 draft pick—but he plans to come back to school.

But as former coach Dean Smith and former player Michael Jordan congratulated them in the

OPPOSITE PAGE: UNC's Sean May powers inside against Illinois' Roger Powell during first-half action during the 2005 NCAA National Basketball Championship.
Staff Photo by Scott Lewis

locker room, they all just wanted to celebrate now while they are a team.

"There were a lot of critics out there," Jawad Williams said. "A team doesn't make it this far, and a team doesn't win a national championship, if they don't play like a team. So we proved a lot of people wrong."

OPPOSITE PAGE TOP: UNC's defense collapses on Illinois' Luther Head in the closing seconds. Raymond Felton, right, stole the ball to seal the 75-70 during the 2005 NCAA National Basketball Championship. *Staff Photo by Ethan Hyman*

OPPOSITE PAGE BOTTOM: UNC seniors Jackie Manuel and Melvin Scott, right, holdovers from the 8-20 team of 2001, jump into each other's arm as time runs out against Illinois during the 2005 NCAA National Basketball Championship. *Staff Photo by Ethan Hyman*

BELOW: UNC players join Roy Williams in hoisting the NCAA Tournament Champions trophy after they defeated Illinois 75-70. *Staff Photo by Scott Lewis*

	1st	2nd	Total
North Carolina	40	35	75
Illinois	27	43	70

NORTH CAROLINA

Player	FGM-A	3FGM-A	FTM-A	O-D REB	A	BLK	S	TP
21 J. Williams	3-6	3-4	0-0	1-4	0	1	1	9
32 McCants	6-15	2-5	0-0	1-1	1	0	1	14
42 May	10-11	0-0	6-8	2-8	2	1	0	26
2 Felton	4-9	4-5	5-6	0-3	7	0	2	17
5 Manuel	0-1	0-0	0-2	0-3	2	0	0	0
1 Scott	0-2	0-1	0-0	0-2	2	0	0	0
3 Terry	0-0	0-0	0-0	0-0	0	0	0	0
11 Thomas	0-0	0-0	0-0	1-0	1	0	0	0
24 M. Williams	4-8	0-1	0-1	3-2	5	0	0	8
34 Noel	0-0	0-0	1-2	1-2	3	0	0	1

ILLINOIS

Player	FGM-A	3FGM-A	FTM-A	O-D REB	A	BLK	S	TP
40 Augustine	0-3	0-0	0-0	1-1	0	0	0	0
43 Powell Jr.	4-10	1-2	0-0	8-6	1	0	1	9
4 Head	8-21	5-16	0-0	1-4	3	1	2	21
5 Williams	7-16	3-10	0-2	0-4	7	0	1	17
11 Brown	4-10	2-8	2-2	0-4	7	0	3	12
33 McBride	0-0	0-0	0-0	0-0	0	0	0	0
41 Carter	0-1	0-1	0-0	1-0	0	0	1	0
45 Smith	0-0	0-0	0-0	0-0	0	0	0	0
50 Ingram	4-9	1-3	2-2	5-2	0	0	0	11

AT LAST AN END TO THE QUESTION

By Caulton Tudor

Forget the national acclaim, the talk-show appearances, the eventual White House visit.

What Roy Williams won on April 4—more than anything else—was an end to all the questions. Maybe now he can talk more about golf, a sport close to his heart.

Talking with reporters one day earlier, Williams was asked roughly two million times about the importance of eventually winning his first national championship.

"I want it, sure," Williams said. "I want it for this team most of all, but I want one of those dadgum things for me, too. I'd like to begin just one season with someone asking how many hole-in-ones I had during the summer rather than how much I need to finally win a championship."

Tee it up, Coach—fire straight at the flag even if it's tucked right next to an alligator-infested pond the size of the Edward Jones Dome.

Williams has his NCAA title. North Carolina has its fourth. Let the lemonade party begin.

Or, as several ecstatic Carolina fans chanted after the game: "One more than Duke! One more than Duke!"

In his fifth Final Four and in his third championship game, Williams finally cracked the elusive code. The magic combination was: 42 left, 2 right, 42 in either direction, or Sean May left, Raymond Felton right, and May from all over.

When it was done, when the Williams watch had ended and the light-blue streamers had exploded from the dome roof onto the Carolina celebration, the coach struggled for just the right words.

"I'm speechless," Williams said. "Usually, I can talk my rear end off, but I'm speechless right now. I'm just so thankful and proud of these players. They took me for a heck of a ride...This is a win for North Carolina's TEAM!"

And a team the Heels were, the team Williams molded in two years with a lot of rich clay left by his former Kansas assistant, Matt Doherty.

But it takes a lot of talent to win a championship. Illinois, which finished 37-2, didn't exactly get here with a group of walk-ons and castoffs.

The Carolina players who came from behind to beat Michigan State in the semifinals Saturday and outlasted the Illini were very much a team, despite widespread suggestions to the contrary. They are now the best team in the country, and they had to prove it the hard way.

This was essentially a road game. The dome was so stocked with orange-clad Illini fans that it looked more like a Clemson home football game on an October Saturday.

There were Tar Heels in the house, sure. Lots of them, including Dean Smith, Michael Jordan, Mitch Kupchak and many more. But for each blue blouse or shirt, there were three in orange.

"The atmosphere for us was great," Illini coach Bruce Weber said. "But they are a tremendous team. They've got great balance...You know, Roy is one of the best in the business."

The great night was the payoff Carolina hoped at some point to realize when Smith finally lured Williams out of Kansas and back to his alma mater.

Of the many postgame embraces exchanged on the court, perhaps the most memorable were the ones involving Williams and athletics director Dick Baddour, and another between Baddour and Chancellor James Moeser.

The thinking when Williams was hired was that he could return the program to the greatness long taken for granted under Smith. Few rational observers expected Williams to manufacture that greatness virtually overnight.

OPPOSITE PAGE: UNC'S Roy Williams celebrates after putting the net around senior Melvin Scott after UNC defeated Illinois 75-70 to win the 2005 National Championship at the Edward Jones Dome in St. Louis. *Staff Photo by Ethan Hyman*

He did, though. Williams sold Rashad McCants, Felton, May, Jawad Williams, David Noel, Jackie Manuel, and Melvin Scott on the importance of unity and dedication to goals.

What we now know is that each of these four Carolina championships has been delivered by exceptional coaches: Frank McGuire in 1957, Smith in '82 and '93—and now the one that marks the foundation of the Ol' Roy era.

ABOVE: UNC head coach Roy Williams watches his team's poor performance against Clemson in their opening game of the ACC tournament. The team shot 38.9% but won the game 88-81. *Staff Photo by Scott Lewis*

OPPOSITE PAGE TOP: UNC coach Roy Williams gathers the three seniors, Melvin Scott, Jawad Williams, and Jackie Manuel after the Tar Heels beat FSU. *Staff Photo by Scott Lewis*

OPPOSITE PAGE BOTTOM: In the second half, UNC's Roy Williams gestures to an official as the Tar Heels beat the University of Connecticut, 77-70. *Staff Photo by Scott Lewis*

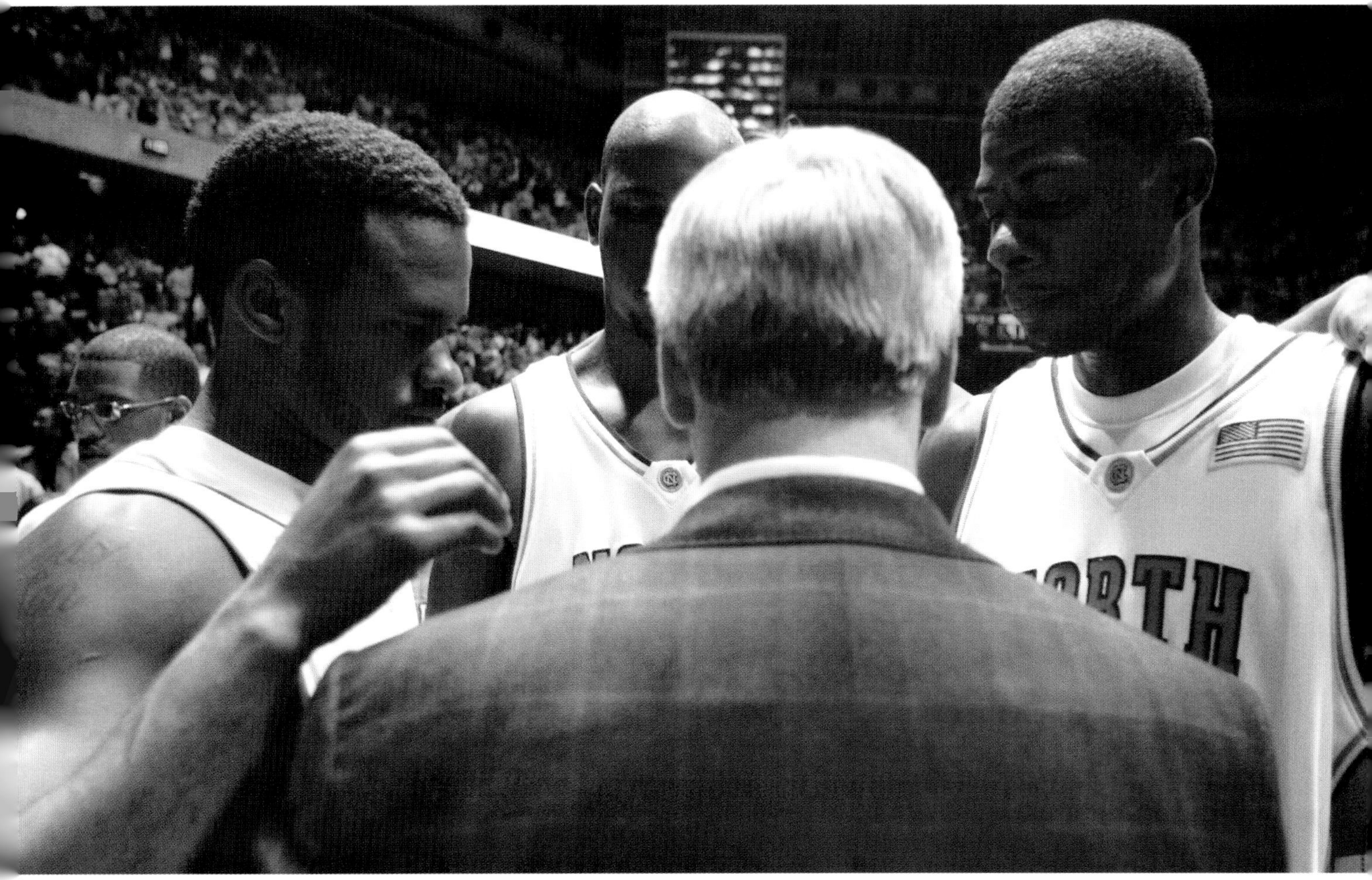
ORTH

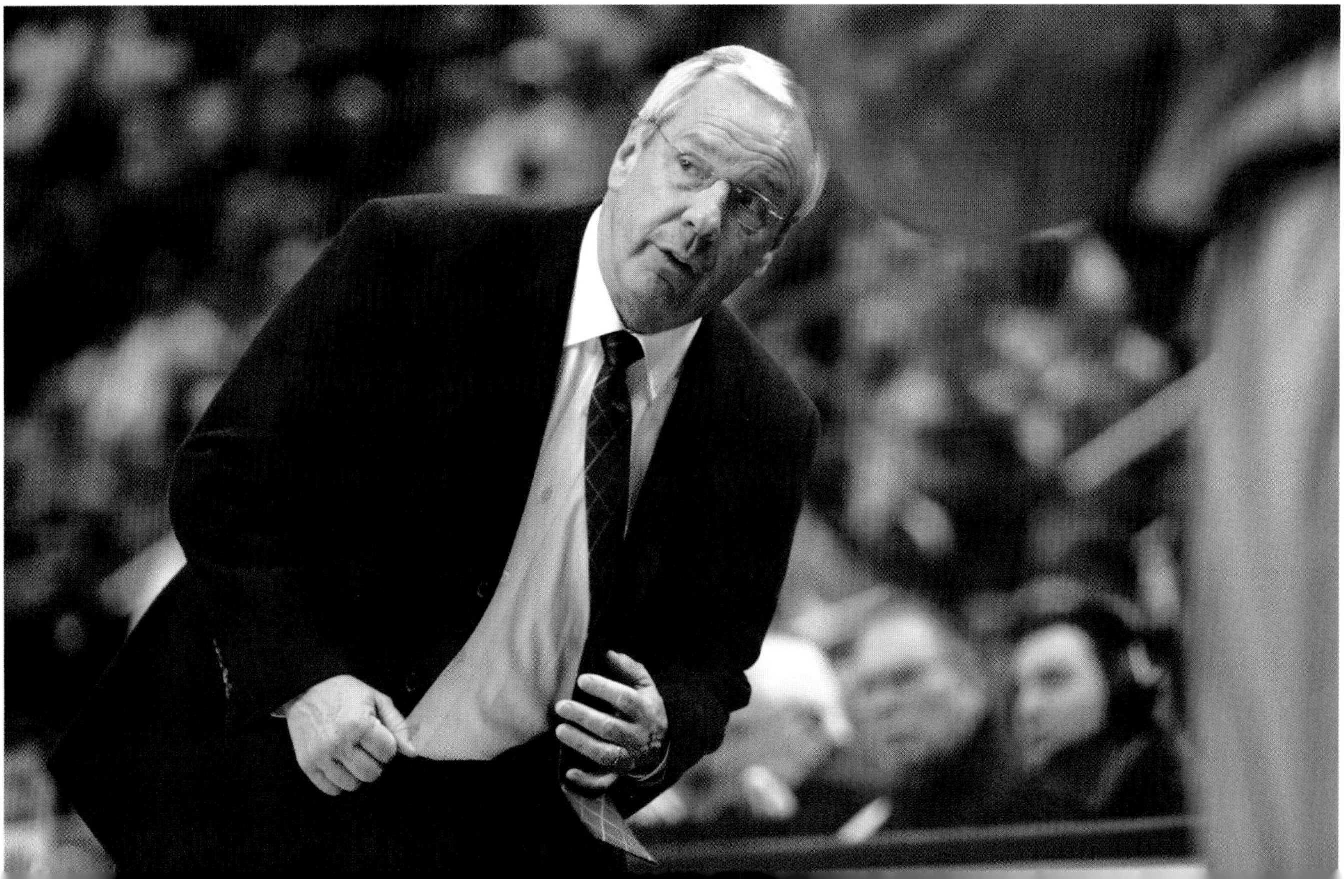

Regular Season Stats

Player	GP	MIN/G	FG%	3-PT%	FT%	REB/G	AST/G	STL/G	BLK/G	PTS	PTS/G
Sean May	37	26.8	.567	.000	.758	10.7	1.7	1.2	1.0	647	17.5
Rashad McCants	33	25.9	.489	.423	.722	3.0	2.7	1.3	0.7	528	16.0
Jawad Williams	37	24.0	.541	.381	.813	4.0	1.4	0.7	0.5	483	13.1
Raymond Felton	36	31.7	.455	.440	.701	4.3	6.9	2.0	0.3	464	12.9
Marvin Williams	36	22.2	.506	.432	.847	6.6	0.7	1.1	0.5	407	11.3
Jackie Manuel	37	21.8	.490	.278	.598	2.8	1.5	1.3	0.3	204	5.5
Melvin Scott	37	16.3	.377	.357	.739	1.4	1.1	0.7	0.1	188	5.1
David Noel	37	16.9	.548	.350	.537	2.6	1.5	0.9	0.3	143	3.9
Reyshawn Terry	32	4.5	.542	.600	.692	0.7	0.2	0.3	0.2	73	2.3
Jesse Holley	10	1.6	.400	.250	.500	0.4	0.2	0.4	0.1	13	1.3
Wes Miller	24	3.8	.300	.313	.692	0.2	0.5	0.0	0.0	26	1.1
Byron Sanders	26	3.0	.455	.000	.200	0.9	0.3	0.0	0.0	22	0.8
Quentin Thomas	37	6.3	.455	.333	.700	0.8	1.3	0.3	0.0	28	0.8
C.J. Hooker	25	2.0	.471	.000	.200	0.5	0.1	0.1	0.0	18	0.7
Charlie Everett	22	2.1	.625	1.000	.333	0.2	0.1	0.0	0.0	12	0.5
Brooks Foster	5	1.8	.000	.000	.333	0.2	0.2	0.4	0.0	1	0.2
Damion Grant	6	2.8	.000	.000	.000	0.7	0.0	0.0	0.0	0	0.0

Regular Season Results

Date	Opponent	Site	Result
Nov. 5	Winston-Salem State (exhibition)	Chapel Hill, NC	W, 113-53
Nov. 12	Mount Olive (exhibition)	Chapel Hill, NC	W, 100-68
Nov. 19	Santa Clara	Oakland, CA	L, 77-66
Nov. 22	BYU	Lahaina, Maui, HI	W, 86-50
Nov. 23	Tennesee	Lahaina, Maui, HI	W, 94-81
Nov. 24	Iowa	Lahaina, Maui, HI	W, 106-92
Nov. 28	USC	Chapel Hill, NC	W, 97-65
Dec. 1	Indiana	Bloomington, IN	W, 70-63
Dec. 4	Kentucky	Chapel Hill, NC	W, 91-78
Dec. 12	Loyola-Chicago	Chapel Hill, NC	W, 109-60
Dec. 19	Virginia Tech	Blacksburg, VA	W, 85-51
Dec. 21	Vermont	Chapel Hill, NC	W, 93-65
Dec. 28	UNC-Wilmington	Chapel Hill, NC	W, 96-75
Dec. 30	Cleveland State	Chapel Hill, NC	W, 107-64
Jan. 2	William & Mary	Chapel Hill, NC	W, 105-66
Jan. 8	Maryland	Chapel Hill, NC	W, 109-75
Jan. 12	Georgia Tech	Chapel Hill, NC	W, 91-69
Jan. 15	Wake Forest	Winston-Salem, NC	L, 95-82
Jan. 19	Clemson	Clemson, SC	W, 77-58
Jan. 22	Miami	Chapel Hill, NC	W, 87-67
Jan. 29	Virginia	Charlottesville, VA	W, 110-76
Feb. 3	North Carolina State	Chapel Hill, NC	W, 95-71
Feb. 6	Florida State	Tallahassee, FL	W, 81-60
Feb. 9	Duke	Durham, NC	L, 71-70
Feb. 13	Connecticut	Hartford, CT	W, 77-70
Feb. 16	Virginia	Chapel Hill, NC	W, 85-61
Feb. 19	Clemson	Chapel Hill, NC	W, 88-56
Feb. 22	North Carolina State	Raleigh, NC	W, 81-71
Feb. 27	Maryland	College Park, MD	W, 85-83
Mar. 3	Florida State	Chapel Hill, NC	W, 91-76
Mar. 6	Duke	Chapel Hill, NC	W, 75-73
Mar. 11	Clemson (ACC Tournament)	Washington, DC	W, 88-81
Mar. 12	Georgia Tech (ACC Tournament)	Washington, DC	L, 78-75
Mar. 18	Oakland (NCAA Tournament)	Charlotte, NC	W, 96-68
Mar. 20	Iowa State (NCAA Tournament)	Charlotte, NC	W, 92-65
Mar. 25	Villanova (NCAA Tournament)	Syracuse, NY	W, 67-66
Mar. 27	Wisconsin (NCAA Tournament)	Syracuse, NY	W, 88-82
Apr. 2	Michigan State (NCAA Tournament)	St. Louis, MO	W, 87-71
Apr. 4	Illinois (NCAA Tournament)	St. Louis, MO	W, 75-70

ACKNOWLEDGMENTS

The entire Staff of *The News & Observer* contributed to the coverage of the 2004-2005 University of North Carolina men's basketball national championship season. The photography, design, graphics, and sports departments did the great bulk of the work.

Photography Department

Photographers
Ethan Hyman, Takaaki Iwabu, Lisa Lauck, Juli Leonard, Scott Lewis, Chuck Liddy, Travis Long, Corey Lowenstein, Harry Lynch, Mel Nathanson, Ted Richardson, Shawn Rocco, John Rottet, Chris Seward, Sher Stoneman, and Robert Willett

Image Technicians
Sam Jones, Kim Kellam, Gail Thrift, and Herman Spencer, Director of Imaging

Picture Editors
Matthew Fortner, John Hansen, Kevin Keister, and Scott Sharpe

Director of Photography
Robert Miller

Graphics Department
Michael Bartes, Judson Drennan, Tim Lee, Frank Medlin, Tom Mosier, and Woody Vondracek

Graphics Editor
Grey Blackwell

Design Desk
Steve Allen, Jon Blasco, Jennifer Bowles, Brian Clement, Al Kraft, Eric Nolen-Weathington, Mike Williams

Assistant Design Editor
Jessaca Giglio

Sports Design Editor
Teresa Kreigsman

Sports Department

Editors
Sherry Johnson, sports editor; Steve Bawden, Dane Huffman, Roger van der Horst, assistant sports editors

Columnists
Ned Barnett and Caulton Tudor

Reporters
Chip Alexander, A.J. Carr, Rachel Carter, Luciana Chavez, Luke DeCock, J.P. Giglio, Lorenzo Perez, Robbi Pickeral, Edward G. Robinson III, Tim Stevens, and Mike Zlotnicki

Copy editors
Tim Blankemeyer, Teri Boggess, Winston Cavin, Ann Kennedy, Gary Mondello, Joe Mustian, Sam Newkirk, Bob Nowell, and Bill Woodward

Sports assistants
Mike Farrell, statistics editor; Nick Ames, Christian Hoyt, Pan Patel, and Lorenzo Phillips